The Objectivity of Judicial Decisions

STUDIES IN POLITICS, SECURITY AND SOCIETY

Edited by Stanisław Sulowski
Institute of Political Science of the University of Warsaw

VOLUME 7

PETER LANG
EDITION

Vito Breda

The Objectivity of Judicial Decisions

A Comparative Analysis of Nine Jurisdictions

PETER LANG
EDITION

Bibliographic Information published by the Deutsche Nationalbibliothek
The Deutsche Nationalbibliothek lists this publication in the Deutsche Nationalbibliografie; detailed bibliographic data is available in the internet at http://dnb.d-nb.de.

This publication was financially supported
by the University of Southern Queensland, Australia.

Library of Congress Cataloging-in-Publication Data
Names: Breda, Vito, 1971-
Title: The objectivity of judicial decisions : a comparative analysis of nine jurisdictions / Vito Breda.
Description: Frankfurt am Main ; New York : Peter Lang, 2017. | Series: Studies in politics, security and society ; vol. 7 | "The data for this project was retrieved from a large sample of cases: over a thousand decisions from Brazil, Hungary, Italy, Lithuania, Slovakia, Slovenia, Spain, Romania and the UK." --Introduction. | Includes bibliographical references and index.
Identifiers: LCCN 2016050393 | ISBN 9783631675908
Subjects: LCSH: Judicial process--Europe. | Bias (Law)--Europe.
Classification: LCC KJC3666 .B74 2017 | DDC 347/.05--dc23 LC record available at https://lccn.loc.gov/2016050393

ISSN 2199-028X
ISBN 978-3-631-67590-8 (Print)
E-ISBN 978-3-631-70211-6 (E-PDF)
E-ISBN 978-3-631-70212-3 (EPUB)
E-ISBN 978-3-631-70213-0 (MOBI)
DOI 10.3726/b10610

Peter Lang Edition is an Imprint of Peter Lang GmbH.

Peter Lang – Frankfurt am Main · Bern · Bruxelles · New York · Oxford · Warszawa · Wien

This publication has been peer reviewed.

www.peterlang.com

Contents

Acknowledgments

This book would not have been possible without the help of Prof Stanislaw Sulowski as the editor of *Studies in Politics, Security and Society* and Peter Lang's exceptionally helpful staff. I am very grateful to my publisher for sticking with me throughout this project. The research benefited from the generous sponsorship by the University of Edinburgh Neil MacCormick's fellowship programme and the USQ Research Division. I have to thank Prof Stephen Tierney for his unparalleled support during the MacCormick's fellowship and Prof Reid Mortensen and Prof Simon Young at the USQ. A special mention has to go to Prof Wagner and the anonymous referees of the International Journal for the Semiotics of Law for their valuable feedback. The author and the publisher are particularly grateful to Springer for the permission to reprint extracts from the article *The Grammar of Bias: Judicial Impartiality in European Legal Systems* published by the International Journal for the Semiotics of Law in August 2016. The research was completed in 2014. The book reports on a large comparative project which involved a group of very gifted and dedicated researchers, who worked over a long period of time and it has been the proxy for several individual and co-authored publications. The list of the individuals involved, with the countries analysed by this article, includes: Maximiliano Aramburo and Sebastian Alonso Agüero San Juan, Michal Pazdziora, Lucia Berdisova, Pietro Denaro, Rūta Kazanavičiūtė, Lidia Rodak, Maciej Pichlak, Jaqueline Sena, Andrej Kristan and Tilen Štajnpihler, Antal Szerletics. Over the years individuals' involvements, as part of the transient nature of legal academia, changed. The first data analysis exercise took place at the 2012 IVR World Congress in Frankfurt. From then, some of the contributors' work has been reviewed and taken over by others. This list is only indicative of the final contributors. The submission complies with COPE guidelines and the Australian Code for the Responsible Conduct of Research. The project's raw data is available for review via the Australia's Academic and Research Network (AARNet). The usual disclaimer applies and so all errors and omissions are the sole responsibility of the author.

Introduction and methodology

1. Modest Objectivity in Judicial Reasoning

The ability to deliver objective, unbiased and just judicial decisions grounded on the truthful representation of the facts is considered an essential aspect of modern liberal democracy.[1] It is so because of multifarious overlapping reasons, yet one of the prominent aspects for considering it the kingpin of modern adjudication is functional.[2] Objectivity is an epistemic requirement of a judicial decision that considers the facts of the case as a truthful representation of past events and that evaluates the range of legal arguments submitted by the parties.[3] This book reports on a large study on the cognitive use of the concept of objectivity, as it has been referred to by the courts, in nine legal systems. The coutries considered were; Brazil, Hungary, Italy, Lithuania, Slovakia, Slovenia, Spain, Romania and the UK. The adopted methodology is the one explained by Langacker's studies on cognitive grammar and it has been tested in other legal studies.[4] The results of the study confirm Legrand's idea of pre-judices in legal discourse.

---

1 Ronald Dworkin, 'Objectivity and Truth: You'd Better Believe It' (1996) 25 Philosophy & Public Affairs 87; Kent Greenawalt, *Law and Objectivity* (Oxford University Press, USA 1995); Richard Rorty, *Objectivity, Relativism, and Truth* (Cambridge University Press 1991); Vito Breda and Lidia Rodak (eds), *Diverse Narratives of Legal Objectivity: An Interdisciplinary Perspective* (Peter Lang 2016); Veronica Rodriguez-Blanco, 'Objectivity in Law' (2010) 5 Philosophy Compass 240; Jules L Coleman and Brian Leiter, 'Determinacy, Objectivity, and Authority' [1993] University of Pennsylvania Law Review 549.

2 Dworkin (n 1) 137; Neil MacCormick, 'Reasonableness and Objectivity' (1998) 74 Notre Dame L. Rev. 1575, 75; Coleman and Leiter (n 1) 590.

3 Neil MacCormick, *Legal Reasoning and Legal Theory* (Clarendon Press 1994) ix.

4 Ronald Langacker, *Foundations of Cognitive Grammar: Volume II: Descriptive Application* (Stanford University Press 1991); Stephen C Levinson, *Pragmatics* (Cambridge University Press 1983); Izabela Skoczeń, 'Minimal Semantics and Legal Interpretation' [2015] International Journal for the Semiotics of Law -; Sol Azuelos-Atias, 'Semantically Cued Contextual Implicatures in Legal Texts' (2010) 42 Journal of Pragmatics 728.

Pre-judices are, according to Legrand, shared cognitive methods that legal practitioners perceive as necessary in a fair and just judicial system.[5]

> These pre-judices (I use the term in its etymological, not in its negative, or acquired, sense) are actively forged, for example, through the schooling process, in which law students are immersed and through which they learn the values, beliefs, dispositions, justifications and the practical consciousness that allows them to consolidate a cultural code, to crystallize their identities and to become professionally socialized.[6]

The existence of cultural variations in judicial practices is a relatively uncontroversial idea,[7] yet there is little known about the effects that pre-judices might have on the judicial narrative and, as proxy, judicial decision.[8]

Studies, such as the one by Azuelos-Atias and Skoczeń, confirmed the existence of cognitive variations within a single legal system.[9] This study, however, is squarely comparative. It is intended to show that a common concept such as objectivity in judicial discourse is constructed by national diverging clusters of significances. The cluster of textual qualifications made by the judicial system is culturally distinctive, rather like human DNA, and it has important pragmatic and theoretical implications.[10] To know the level of cognitive distinctiveness of a legal system is, for instance, essential for the

---

5 Pierre Legrand, 'European Legal Systems Are Not Converging' (1996) 45 The International and Comparative Law Quarterly 52, 51.

6 Legrand (n 5) 51. For a general analysis of comparative law as a cultural artefact, see: Günter Frankenberg, 'How to Do Projects with Comparative Law - Notes of an Expedition to the Common Core' (2006) 6 Global Jurist Advances.

7 H Patrick Glenn, *Legal Traditions of the World: Sustainable Diversity in Law* (Oxford University Press 2010); Steven J Burton, *The Path of the Law and Its Influence: The Legacy of Oliver Wendell Holmes, Jr.* (Cambridge University Press 2000).

8 Skoczeń (n 4); Marek Zirk-Sadowski, 'Interpretation of Law and Judges Communities' (2012) 25 International Journal for the Semiotics of Law - 473; Azuelos-Atias (n 4); Breda and Rodak (n 1).

9 Skoczeń (n 4); Alberto Abadie and Javier Gardeazabal, 'The Economic Costs of Conflict: A Case Study of the Basque Country' (2003) 93 The American Economic Review 113.

10 Conceptually, this analogy could be taken further perhaps in future studies. For example, even when a gene has been knocked out, a supportive and nourishing environment means that a skill can be re-learnt. The dilemma would be whether judicial training schemes might alter the effect of legal culture.

implementation of large ambitious plans such as a constitution for Europe or for the implementation of policies that fight organised, multinational criminal activities.[11] These types of coordinated activities often assume the existence of a shared understanding of general legal concepts. The study shows that, even at the lexical level, all of the legal systems considered in this study are semantically distinctive and that a series of national pre-judices fills general concepts such as objectivity, independence, justice and fairness with their respective functional significance. Acknowledging this range of pre-judices has, it could reasonably be argued, direct implications in terms of the implementation of international treaties, the functioning of multinational organisations such as the European Union and the plausibility of large international harmonisation projects.[12]

The evidence of a range of cognitive activities perceived as objective by a national community of legal practitioners also has effects on the theoretical assumptions of the analytical jurisprudence of, for instance, Hart[13] and of nihilist analyses that are distinctive of the Critical Legal Studies (CLS) movement.[14] For instance, Hart has defended his idea of narrow discretion in law as part of an analysis on the separation between law and morals. The possibility of judges being able to select a method from a range of available cognitive approaches with which to provide the 'best' answer to

11 Pierre Legrand, 'Against a European Civil Code' (1997) 60 The Modern Law Review 44, 50. V Breda, 'A European Constitution in a Multinational Europe or a Multinational Constitution for Europe?' (2006) 12 European Law Journal 330; Annelise Anderson, 'Organised Crime, Mafia and Governments' in Sam Peltzman and Gianluca Fiorentini (eds), *The Economics of Organised Crime* (Cambridge University Press 1997).

12 Legrand (n 5); Reinhard Zimmermann, 'Civil Code and Civil Law - The Europeanization of Private Law within the European Community and the Re-Emergence of a European Legal Science' (1994) 1 Columbia Journal of European Law 63; Eckart Brodermann, 'International Contract and Arbitration Practice-The Experience of a German Lawyer' (2011) 16 Uniform Law Review. 589.

13 HLA Hart, *The Concept of Law* (Penelope Bulloch and Joseph Raz eds, 2nd edition, Oxford University Press 1997); HLA Hart, 'Positivism and the Separation of Law and Morals' (1958) 71 Harvard Law Review 593; HLA Hart, *Essays in Jurisprudence and Philosophy* (Oxford University Press 1983).

14 Costas Douzinas and Adam Gearey, *Critical Jurisprudence: The Political Philosophy of Justice* (Hart 2005); Emilios Christodoulidis, *Law and Reflexive Politics* (Kluwer 1998).

a legal dilemma indicates the existence of a level of external indeterminacy in judicial reasoning. In other words, even in an ideal epistemic condition in which a judge has a truthful representation of the facts of the case and has mastered all the legal expertise of Dworkin's Herculean judge, she might still have the possibility of being able to choose from one among the many different available cognitive methods in order to reach her decision. The chosen epistemic method, it is reasonable to assume, might condition the outcome of the case.[15]

So, the study shows evidence of a range of perceived 'right' cognitive legal methods, yet the indication that there are multiple contextual epistemic methods associated with the idea of judicial objectivity does not provide a *tout court* argument against the role of positivism in judicial reasoning.[16] It supports, instead, the existence of a modest concept of objectivity.[17] The idea of modest objectivity in legal reasoning has been qualified by Leiter and Coleman. They suggest the existence of three types of epistemic practices in judicial reasoning called *strong*, *modest* and *weak* or *minimal*.[18] The first group of cognitive activities is normally associated with the scientific method adopted in natural science. DNA and ballistic reports result from *hard* epistemic practices that seek to provide a verifiable representation of past events such as the cause of death of a victim.[19] The scientific method is the best known of all scientific epistemologies and it is also one of the most contested.[20] The polemic associated with the nihilist critique of legal reasoning will be discussed in several parts of this book, but at this stage, I will simply say that the study has found little evidence of the ideological colonisation of judicial reasoning.[21]

---

15 Ronald Dworkin, *Law's Empire* (Hart 1998) 239.

16 MacCormick (n 3) 100. It was outside the remit of this study to discuss whether, and if the answer was in the positive how, legal narratives affect outcomes.

17 Coleman and Leiter (n 1).

18 Coleman and Leiter (n 1) 559, 592.

19 Coleman and Leiter (n 1) 571.

20 Rorty (n 1); Thomas S Kuhn, *The Structure of Scientific Revolutions: 50th Anniversary Edition* (University of Chicago Press 2012).

21 Breda and Rodak (n 1); Vito Breda, 'The Grammar of Bias: Judicial Impartiality in European Legal Systems' [2016] International Journal for the Semiotics of Law -.

Weak epistemic practices might instead be associated with the subjective and unconstrained analysis of a literary composition or an art piece.[22] Judicial reasoning is a modestly objective cognitive activity that combines factual narratives and an interpretative activity.[23] Again, Coleman and Leiter deliver a clear explanation of the benefits of associating positivism with a modest concept of objectivity.

> Modest objectivity allows the possibility that everybody could be wrong about what a rule requires; what seems right even to everyone about what a rule requires may not be right. Only what seems right to individuals placed in an epistemically ideal position determines what is right. At the same time, modest objectivity provides a sense in which sentences can be objective that does not depend on their truth-conditions being fully independent of our epistemic resources and access to them.[24]

By recognising the intrinsic limitations of legal reasoning, Coleman and Leiter's modest objectivity escapes the strong realist critique of, for instance, Rorty.[25] Courts could, indeed, choose from among a series of cognitive methods and such a choice might alter the outcome of the case, yet the decision will be considered as objective in a legal positive sense because the process conforms to the accepted orthopraxy.

The sample of cases considered in this study includes instances in which courts evaluated an allegation of bias. In cases in which there is an allegation of objective bias, the decision to transfer a case or to allow an appeal focused almost exclusively on factual narratives. The case might be decided by accepting the result of a report by a financial forensic expert who proved a monetary interest in the case by the judge who had been called to make a decision on the case.[26] The shared reference to a scientific method and the consistency of the decisions in cases of allegations of objective judicial bias, which might support the ideal of determinacy in judicial reasoning, is not replicated in allegations of subjective judicial bias.[27] In these types of cases,

22 Coleman and Leiter (n 1) 577; Dworkin (n 14) 6.
23 Coleman and Leiter (n 1) 512.
24 Coleman and Leiter (n 1) 621.
25 Rorty (n 1).
26 Table One Group C, subgroup f, Breda, 'The Grammar of Bias: Judicial Impartiality in European Legal Systems' (n 20).
27 Dworkin (n 14) Chapter 6.

the study found that each national legal system relies on large clusters of cognitive methods.[28] For instance, the House of Lords considered an intersubjective perception of subjective bias in R v Bow Street Metropolitan Stipendiary Magistrate Ex p Pinochet Ugarte (No2) as sufficient to deem Lord Hoffmann's indirect involvement with Amnesty International as pernicious of the entire decision.[29] It is important to note that in R v Bow Street Metropolitan Stipendiary Magistrate Ex p Pinochet Ugarte (No2) there is no evidence that Lord Hoffmann's contribution to the case was biased, yet the House of Lords, by making reference to the intersubjective criteria of the reasonable person, upheld the appeal. In contrast to the criterion of the perception of the reasonable person, an allegation of subjective bias in Lithuania requires that a personal allegation of bias is coupled with a procedural impropriety.[30] The different epistemic methods adopted in the two legal systems that I assume support different judicial outcomes are perceived by the majority of the national community of legal professionals as 'objective'. They are, in other words, a manifestation of a segment of cognitive methods that each legal community associated with an objective decision.

There is an overlap between Legrand's idea of pre-judices in European judicial systems and Coleman and Leiter's idea of modest objectivity in law.[31] From an internal-to-the-judiciary point of view, the decision of Vilnius Regional Court No. 1A-543-209-2011 and the outcome of R v Bow Street Metropolitan Stipendiary Magistrate Ex p Pinochet Ugarte (No2) are the logical result of a cognitive activity that is perceived as correct by the respective national communities of legal practitioners. A comparative analysis that focuses on external functional expectations based on, for instance, an Italian ethnocentric perspective of the rule against bias, might suggest that both decisions are unacceptable.[32] However, a broader comparison,

28 Table One, Group C.

29 *R v Bow Street Metropolitan Stipendiary Magistrate Ex p Pinochet Ugarte (No2) [2000]* (1999) 1 AC 119 (HL); Kerry Abadee, 'Lessons from the Pinochet Case for the Bias Rule of Procedural Fairness in Its Application to Australian Judges' 8 Journals, Australian Journal of Administrative Law 19.

30 Vilnius Regional Court No. 1A-543-209-2011.

31 Legrand (n 10) 51; Coleman and Leiter (n 1).

32 Vito Breda and Matteo Vricella, 'English Pragmatism and Italian Virtue: A Comparative Analysis of the Regime of Illegally Obtained Evidence in Civil

such as the one discussed in this book, shows that all the judicial systems considered in this book seek to reduce the pernicious effects of bias. The cognitive methods that each legal system implements to mitigate the effect of the subjective relation between the parties and a judge must be within the range of epistemic methods that a community of legal practitioners perceives as appropriate.

In the UK, for instance, a perception of bias might be sufficient for a successful appeal, whereas in Lithuania, a party alleging a judicial interest in a dispute has to make manifest a procedural violation. However, in both instances, the cognitive activity associated with both allegations is narrowed by the expectation that the court will reasonably comply with the existing practice and will consider the long-term implications of its decision.[33] Hart, for instance, describes the cognitive activity expected from judges in a legal system that complies with the cannons of positivism as reasoned 'choices between alternatives'.[34] The cognitive choice is not a mechanical application of sovereign power, as a conventionalist might perceive it to be, or subjective, as the CLS movement has suggested.[35] The cognitive process is an attempt to deliver an objective description of the facts of the case that meet with an interpretative activity of the rule. The qualification of a choice between alternatives is in tune with the idea of modest objectivity, as defined by Coleman and Leiter, and can be extended to legal positivism.[36]

The results of this study show that judicial reasoning is modestly objective. For instance, Zucca's comparative analysis of the right of privacy across Europe and the USA shows large variations in how judges balance that right against freedom of speech.[37] According to Zucca, the indeterminacy could

---

Law Proceedings between Italy and England' (2014) 21 Maastricht journal of European and comparative law 428.

33 MacCormick (n 3) 87.

34 Hart, 'Positivism and the Separation of Law and Morals' (n 12) 612.

35 Hart, *The Concept of Law* (n 12) 1–2; Douzinas and Gearey (n 13).

36 Coleman and Leiter (n 1).

37 Lorenzo Zucca, *Constitutional Dilemmas: Conflicts of Fundamental Legal Rights in Europe and the USA* (Oxford University Press 2007) 97; Vito Breda, 'Constitutional Dilemmas: Conflicts of Fundamental Legal Rights in Europe and the USA by Lorenzo Zucca' (2009) 72 The Modern Law Review 325.

be resolved by introducing more procedural rules.[38] Indeed, clear and specific rules regarding the procedural accommodation of constitutional dilemmas might appease the conventionalists. However, these rules might not be perceived as legitimate by the community of legal professionals who are trusted with the task of applying them, and even if they were, a national cluster of cognitive activities associated with an objective interpretation would continue to support the legitimacy of the aforementioned national variations. Zucca's conclusion is well articulated and it might have the merit of showing the importance of cognitive activities that seek to qualify the accommodation of constitutional claims, but the results of the study discussed in this book suggest that clearer 'procedural rules' are unlikely to alter the national perceptions of legitimacy and objectivity.[39]

2. Objectivity: a second order of justification

Zucca's comparative analysis might not be confirmed by this study, yet empirical studies seldom bring good news to the supporters of conventional jurisprudence. This study is no exception. The realist critique of positivism has derived much of its strength from empirical studies which show the indeterminacy in, for instance, sentencing.[40] Empirical studies also fuelled feminist and critical race studies' narratives.[41] However, this project, which focused on the lexical qualification of the concept of objectivity by judges, suggests that courts seek to deliver unbiased just decisions that are perceived as a manifestation of a fair and just society by the national community of

38 Breda, 'Constitutional Dilemmas' (n 36) 169.

39 Breda, 'Constitutional Dilemmas' (n 36) 179.

40 Shai Danziger, Jonathan Levav and Liora Avnaim-Pesso, 'Extraneous Factors in Judicial Decisions' (2011) 108 Proceedings of the National Academy of Sciences of the United States of America 6889; Alex Kozinski, 'What I Ate for Breakfast and Other Mysteries of Judicial Decision Making' (1992) 26 Loy. LAL Rev. 993; Brian Leiter, 'Legal Realism and Legal Positivism Reconsidered*' (2001) 111 Ethics 278.

41 Oren Gazal-Ayal and Raanan Sulitzeanu-Kenan, 'Let My People Go: Ethnic In-Group Bias in Judicial Decisions—Evidence from a Randomized Natural Experiment' (2010) 7 Journal of Empirical Legal Studies 403; Gillian Douglas, Julia Pearce and Hilary Woodward, 'Cohabitants, Property and the Law: A Study of Injustice' (2009) 72 Modern Law Review 24.

legal practitioners.[42] Objectivity is one of the requirements of a judicial decision under ideal epistemic conditions. The study, however, sought to flesh out the cognitive assumptions that judges across different legal systems consider essential to an objective decision.[43]

As deduced by Coleman and Leiter, the results of the study show little indication of ideological bias or of judges being aware of using intersubjective concepts to deliver their decisions. Only in two cases (out of over a thousand considered in this book) did a party allege that the court was ideologically biased.[44] Of course this might not repeal the claim that judges are part of the same Boy's Club. An assessment of the results of this project suggests, instead, that a second order of justifications in legal reasoning, which is described by positivists such as MacCormick as neutral, is a manifestation of national sociological preferences.[45]

MacCormick argues that the epistemic methods adopted in legal systems are not fundamentally different from the ones used in natural science.[46] He refers directly to Popper's qualification of the scientific method in natural science.[47] The requirement of legal reasoning is, MacCormick continues, to provide a meaningful justification for a rule that has a normative connotation.[48] The epistemic dichotomy, he concludes, between the natural explanation of reality and a normative 'ought' in legal reasoning is false since both processes require a plausible justification. He provides, I think, one of the most eloquent explanations of the normative underpinning of legal reasoning: 'Legal rulings are normative; they do not report, they *set* patterns of behaviours; they do not discover the consequences of given conditions,

---

42 Coleman and Leiter (n 1) 636–637.

43 David Dyzenhaus, *Hard Cases in Wicked Legal Systems: Pathologies of Legality* (Oxford University Press 2010) 14, 187.; Hart, *The Concept of Law* (n 12) postscript.

44 Budapest Metropolitan Court No. 27.P. 24.578/2006./3, Supreme Court of Lithuania (CLS) case No. 3K-3-93/2011.

45 MacCormick (n 3) 100, 103.; Maksymilian Del Mar, 'The Forward-Looking Requirement of Formal Justice: Neil MacCormick on Consequential Reasoning' (2015) 6 Jurisprudence 429.

46 MacCormick (n 3) 103; Karl Popper, *The Logic of Scientific Discovery* (Routledge 2005).

47 MacCormick (n 3) 102.

48 MacCormick (n 3) 104.

they ordain what consequences *are* to follow upon given conditions. They do not present a model *of* the world; they present a model *for* it.'[49] So, legal reasoning ought to be normative, and adopting objective epistemic practice is, it is reasonable to argue, one of its normative requirements.

As I mentioned earlier, the possibility of a normative connection between objectivity and legal reasoning in liberal societies is deeply contested, but MacCormick's analyses conceded (like Hart, Coleman and Leiter) that judicial decisions include choosing between rival models of human conduct.[50] However, MacCormick introduces a *consequentialist mode of argument* as one of the normative criteria that judges ought to use to mitigate the effect of subjective perception. Judicial reasoning includes, according to MacCormick, an evaluation of the effect of a decision in analogous cases. He called this second order of justification *universalisability*,[51] and this involves an assessment of the coherency of the decision with pre-existing common law rules and principles.[52] There are, however, strong indications that a consequentialist method might be limited to common law jurisdictions.[53] For instance, the effects of illegally obtained evidence in a trial are part of a consequentialist evaluation in England, but they are perceived *a priori* as antithetical with the deontological aims of a just legal system in Italy.[54] On a general level, the study of the lexical qualification of judicial objectivity confirmed that a second order of justifications is based on intersubjective epistemic practices identifiable as national pre-judices.[55] Judges in the legal systems considered in this study (which includes the jurisprudence of the UK Supreme Court) do refer to the concept of objectivity as a normative requirement of legal reasoning, but its qualification generates a cluster of intersubjective narratives. These narratives are distinctive of a national legal system.

A careful reading of *Legal Reasoning* shows that MacCormick acknowledged the intersubjective nature of judicial choices,[56] yet the requirement

49 MacCormick (n 3) 104.
50 MacCormick (n 3) 104.
51 MacCormick (n 3) 87.
52 MacCormick (n 3) 118.
53 Breda and Vricella (n 31); Del Mar (n 44).
54 Breda and Vricella (n 31).
55 Legrand (n 10) 51; Legrand (n 5).
56 MacCormick (n 3) 101–104.

of *universalisability* purported from those assumptions appears to be tangential from his deduction.[57] The intersubjective limits of MacCormick's *universalisability* are particularly clear in his analysis of the relationship between judicial objectivity and the intersubjective concept of the reasonable person.[58] The connection between the two concepts is constructed as an axiomatic element of the common law that MacCormick defined as 'a pragmatic external view of a legal issue'.[59] However, a reference to an 'external observer' is not sufficient to qualify a legal reasoning as objective. The reasonable person cannot be associated with a detached spectator in a scientific experiment who has the task of reporting the results from digital instruments. Instead, the judicial concept of a reasonable person is an epistemic device that judges use to evaluate the persuasiveness of factual or legal narratives. MacCormick provides a series of examples in which, for instance, the court adopts the criterion of reasonableness to limit contractual liability.[60] The conclusion, he admits, resembles a Hezekiah–Sennacherib narrative in which the author seeks to deduce a conclusion from diverging examples.[61]

Yet, the bathos is followed by a remarkable assertion: 'What is required is attention to, and deliberation over, the relative human importance of the different factors that enter the judgement in any given case.'[62] In other words, the concept of the reasonable person, as a qualifier of judicial objectivity, is a procedural aspect of the decision that judges use to carry out what is, in the end, an intersubjective evaluation.

For instance, the sample of cases taken from the jurisprudence of the UK Supreme Court shows that British judges sometimes coupled the concept of reasonableness and objectivity, but it was more common to consider the objectivity associated with a scientific analysis.[63] So, it is possible to conclude

57 Del Mar (n 44).
58 MacCormick (n 2).
59 MacCormick (n 2) 1579.
60 MacCormick (n 2) 1594.
61 MacCormick (n 2) 1603.
62 MacCormick (n 2) 1603.
63 Vito Breda, 'The Concept of Objectivity in the UK Supreme Court Through a Comparative Looking Glass' in Vito Breda and Lidia Rodak (eds), *Diverse narratives of legal objectivity: an interdisciplinary perspective* (Peter Lang 2016).

that, first, British judges do link the reasonableness to judicial objectivity, but that such a connection is one of the many epistemic methods adopted to qualify their role as independent evaluators, and second, that the concept of reasonableness is a manifestation of a national pre-judice and not a second order of normative justifications as proposed by MacCormick.[64]

3. Research methods and assumptions

In the previous sections, I explained that each legal system adopts a series of cognitive activities which are associated with the concept of objectivity. The result has both pragmatic and theoretical implications. The result was based on the analysis of a large sample of cases. The issue in this type of study is how much someone can bite off without losing significant data or being overwhelmed by variables.[65] For instance, the study focused exclusively on judicial qualifications of the concept of objectivity. To ensure a sufficient breadth of material, the project also evaluated how the concept of objectivity was qualified by dependent concepts such as bias, truth, discretion and justice. In the early stages of this project, it was decided that plausible answers to the research questions required several judicial systems, an uncategorised sample of cases and a large amount of data.[66]

The project involved over twelve researchers and two coordinators. All of the individual researchers had the linguistic and legal training necessary to analyse a large sample of random cases. I coordinated the final review of the data and provided one of the national reports. Each researcher had to report on a sample of cases (at least one hundred cases) in which the court explicitly qualified the concept of judicial objectivity.[67] The analysis was carried out in two stages. In the first stage, the researchers were required to classify the types of lexical qualifications of the concept of objectivity. This was a 'quasi-mechanical' task without the direct use of the Natural

64 MacCormick (n 3) 100.

65 Azuelos-Atias (n 4); Zirk-Sadowski (n 8).

66 Skoczeń (n 4).

67 The project's raw data is available for review via the Australia's Academic and Research Network (AARNet).

Language Tool Kit software.[68] In most, but not all legal systems, the sample of cases was retrieved from an electronic database. The legal systems that were analysed included the Brazilian, Hungarian, Italian, Lithuanian, Slovakian, Slovenian, Spanish, Romanian and the British legal systems. The jurisprudence of the European Court of Justice was also analysed but the results did not produce an appreciable cluster of significances. It is outside the remit of this book to discuss the implications of such results yet, it is important to note that a lack of similarity between the qualifications of the concept of judicial objectivity by an international tribunal does not disprove the existence of national pre-judices.

In the first stage, the researchers had to extract the text in which the court qualified the concept of objectivity. A questionnaire was designed to help individual researchers in this task.[69] The extracts consist of legal textual references to the concept of objectivity without considering their full co-textual significance.[70] The co-textual aspects of language are, according to Levinson, a series of cognitive activities that is carried out by the recipient of an utterance. Skoczeń provides one of the clearest examples of the interplay between textual meaning and co-textual significance: 'A, B and C are standing in front of a lake. A points toward the water and says: A. Look! A hippo's head! B. Oh! It is. C. It's probably a whole hippo; it's just that the rest of him is under the water.' The process of evaluation that is manifested in C delivers the comic punchline because it shows that C refuses to acknowledge the subsumed co-textual information that hippos' heads are normally attached to their bodies.[71] In the first part of the research, investigators grouped the lexical qualifications of the concept of objectivity by only making use of their lexical references.

---

68 'Natural Language Toolkit — NLTK 3.0 Documentation' <http://www.nltk.org/> accessed 3 June 2016.

69 Copies of the questionnaires are available for review via the Australia's Academic and Research Network (AARNet).

70 Azuelos-Atias (n 4); Maj-Britt Mosegaard Hansen, 'On the Availability of "literal" Meaning: Evidence from Courtroom Interaction' (2008) 40 Journal of Pragmatics 1392; Ronald W Langacker, *Language and Its Structure: Some Fundamental Linguistic Concepts* (Harcourt, Brace & World 1968) 84; Langacker, *Foundations of Cognitive Grammar* (n 4).

71 Skoczeń (n 4) 7.

The data at this stage included scrawling verbiage in which the words *objectivity*, *objectively*, or *objective* carried a limited reference to their lexical significance. However, the majority of usages of the concept of objectivity were associated with distinctive cognitive functions. This was expected. Legal discourse is an eminently pragmatic activity carried out with and by public officials with limited resources.[72]

The second stage of the study included a contextual analysis of the *extracts*. This activity had the aim of *labelling* their lexical use.[73] In this part of the research, the investigators had to consider the cognitive activity that the court had undertaken in its attempt to qualify the concept of objectivity. For instance, the text of the case could read: 'The traces of DNA retrieved on the bedsheet are an objective confirmation of the suspect's whereabouts.' The chosen extract was then included in the sub-group of narratives that associated judicial objectivity with factual narratives. The connection between the result of a scientific activity and the court's qualification of such an activity as objective provides a description of the lexical association but, in the first stage of the study, it is reported without considering *contextual information*.

In the second stage of this assessment, the investigators were asked to qualify the type of cognitive activity that the court carried out in the particular case. In the case of 'traces of DNA retrieved on the bedsheet', the court carried out an evaluation of evidence that sought to disprove the implications of finding the DNA and concluded that the traces of DNA objectively indicated the presence of an individual in the bedroom. The cognitive activity carried out by the court was classified as an *evaluation* of the factual narratives.

A variety of methodological assumptions informed the qualification of the type of cognitive activity carried out by the court. The project relied, in particular, on Langacker's study of grammar. Langacker argues that lexical concepts such as *freedom* can be better understood as a cluster of cognitive activities that are normally associated with such concepts.[74] So, a study that

72 Azuelos-Atias (n 4).

73 Skoczeń (n 4).

74 Langacker, *Foundations of Cognitive Grammar* (n 4); Ronald W Langacker, *Cognitive Linguistics Research [CLR]: Concept, Image, and Symbol: The Cognitive Basis of Grammar (2)* (De Gruyter Mouton 1990) ch 1.

intends to clarify the role of a particular concept should also consider the cluster of concepts that are normally associated with the target concept. For instance, the study discovered that the concept of judicial objectivity is often associated with the independence of expert witnesses who are also 'civil servants'. The concept of independence of the civil servants is also psychologically associated with the idea of the transparency of public institutions and so on. The key advantage of Langacker's idea of cognitive activities, such as evaluating or describing a claim, is that it allows for the possibility of studying a network of concepts across linguistic barriers.

After the first comparative data analysis at the 2012 IVR World Congress in Frankfurt, it was relatively clear that a comparative analysis of judicial objectivity could not merely focus on minimal lexical significances, such as was suggested by Borg.[75] In particular, it was fair to assume that even if English were a common language among the project investigators, the existence of a common idiom would not compensate for the national linguistic variations.[76] For instance, Borg's decontextualised lexical studies and Eco's studies on semiotics might provide a complete analysis of the lexical significances of the term *objectivity* within a legal system.[77] Skoczeń provides one of the most extensive analyses of the benefits and the shortcomings of Borg's methodological approaches.[78] However, to be compared, each national cluster of lexical significances obtained in this manner would have to be translated into a common language and the process of translating significance would necessarily have to include a contextual assessment by the individuals who translated it.[79] To reduce the contextual element of the translation's effect, the national results would have to be translated by bilingual mother tongue English speakers (e.g. British approved legal translators). The results of these translations would have produced a mindboggling

75 Emma Borg, *Minimal Semantics* (Clarendon 2004).

76 Nicholas Evans and Stephen C Levinson, 'The Myth of Language Universals: Language Diversity and Its Importance for Cognitive Science' (2009) 32 Behavioral and Brain Sciences 429.

77 Borg (n 77); Umberto Eco, *The Open Work* (Harvard University Press 1989).

78 Skoczeń (n 4); Sol Azuelos-Atias, 'Semantically Cued Contextual Implicatures in Legal Texts' (2010) 42 Journal of Pragmatics 728.

79 Evans and Levinson (n 78).

number of lexical meanings which, due to the range of cultural variables, would have yielded very few scientific outcomes.

However, the aim of the study was not to search for an implausible, minimal common legal definition (or a series of common lexical definitions) of the concept of objectivity. The project's aim was, instead, to verify the existence of cultural variations in the concept of judicial objectivity from among a series of relatively large legal systems. Langacker's methodology allowed national investigators to focus on the matrix of cognitive activities associated with the concept of objectivity that, as with any other epistemic endeavour, could be the object of comparison.[80]

Table 1, at the end of this book, provides a graphic representation of the national matrix of cognitive uses of the concept of objectivity. A quick glance reveals that each judicial system has its own cluster of concepts associated with the term *objectivity*. The ductility of the concept of objectivity confirmed the theoretical assumptions of Coleman and Leiter's idea of modest objectivity in law.[81] It also confirmed Legrand's deductive reasoning which suggests that each legal system has its own set of pre-judices that is perceived, at the very least, as acceptable by the relevant community of legal professionals.[82]

The book is divided into four chapters. The first chapter discusses the network of cognitive uses of the term *objectivity* in cases in which the courts review an allegation of judicial bias. The analysis focuses on cases in which a party makes objective and subjective allegations of judicial bias. An objective allegation of bias suggests that the judge has a direct interest in the issues upon which s/he is called to decide. A personal allegation of bias suggests that a judge might have a personal or professional connection with one of the parties.

The second chapter analyses the interplay between the concepts of objectivity, truth and justice in the judicial narrative. The concept of truth, in legal discourse, is normally associated with procedural truth. That is a choreographed representation of the facts of the case that is in compliance with the

80 Langacker, *Foundations of Cognitive Grammar* (n 4); Ronald W Langacker, *Investigations in Cognitive Grammar* (De Gruyter Mouton 2009).

81 Coleman and Leiter (n 1).

82 Legrand (n 10).

rules regulating evidence submission. The chapter shows a large variation by national courts in the use of the concept of objectivity as a qualifier of a truthful representation of the facts. The Italian sample of cases, for instance, confirmed the existence of Taruffo's verophobia. Tarruffo argued that a large section of the Italian judiciary mechanically upholds deontological principles that hinder the functioning of the civil justice system. The chapter reports on how the concept of justice is normally associated with three distinctive cognitive uses. The first group of judicial narratives focused on procedural justice. The second group of significances considered justice as an equitable solution to a dispute. The last group of judicial narratives sought for a way in which to allocate public resources in an equitable manner.

Chapter Three discusses cases in which the judges had reasonable discretion and referred to the concept of objectivity. Thus, Chapter Three discusses the range of epistemic methods that judges adopt in cases in which there is no predetermined explicit legal rule. These are cases, for instance, in which the court is asked to decide which expert witness report, from among several, is to be considered as binding. On the linear scale that connects hard cases with difficult cases, judicial discretion cases tend to be closer to the former than to the latter. Distinctive to objective discretion cases is the rhetorical use of the concept of objectivity.

Chapter Four presents a commentary on the results of the project represented in Table 1. Table 1 provides an accessible comparison of the legal systems considered in the project which intended to map how courts lexically and cognitively construct the concept of judicial objectivity.

Bibliography

Abadee K, 'Lessons from the Pinochet Case for the Bias Rule of Procedural Fairness in Its Application to Australian Judges' 8 Journals, Australian Journal of Administrative Law 19

Abadie A and Gardeazabal J, 'The Economic Costs of Conflict: A Case Study of the Basque Country' (2003) 93 The American Economic Review 113

Anderson A, 'Organised Crime, Mafia and Governments' in Sam Peltzman and Gianluca Fiorentini (eds), *The Economics of Organised Crime* (Cambridge University Press 1997)

Azuelos-Atias S, 'Semantically Cued Contextual Implicatures in Legal Texts' (2010) 42 Journal of Pragmatics 728

_, 'Semantically Cued Contextual Implicatures in Legal Texts' (2010) 42 Journal of Pragmatics 728

Borg E, *Minimal Semantics* (Clarendon 2004)

Breda V, 'A European Constitution in a Multinational Europe or a Multinational Constitution for Europe?' (2006) 12 European Law Journal 330

Breda V, 'Constitutional Dilemmas: Conflicts of Fundamental Legal Rights in Europe and the USA by Lorenzo Zucca' (2009) 72 The Modern Law Review 325

_, 'The Concept of Objectivity in the UK Supreme Court Through a Comparative Looking Glass' in Vito Breda and Lidia Rodak (eds), *Diverse narratives of legal objectivity: an interdisciplinary perspective* (Peter Lang 2016)

_, 'The Grammar of Bias: Judicial Impartiality in European Legal Systems' [2016] International Journal for the Semiotics of Law -

Breda V and Rodak L (eds), *Diverse Narratives of Legal Objectivity: An Interdisciplinary Perspective* (Peter Lang 2016)

Breda V and Vricella M, 'English Pragmatism and Italian Virtue: A Comparative Analysis of the Regime of Illegally Obtained Evidence in Civil Law Proceedings between Italy and England' (2014) 21 Maastricht Journal of European and Comparative Law 428

Brodermann E, 'Impact of the UNIDROIT Principles on International Contract and Arbitration Practice-The Experience of a German Lawyer.' (2011) 16 Uniform Law Review 589

Burton SJ, *The Path of the Law and Its Influence: The Legacy of Oliver Wendell Holmes, Jr.* (Cambridge University Press 2000)

Christodoulidis E, *Law and Reflexive Politics* (Kluwer 1998)

Coleman JL and Leiter B, 'Determinacy, Objectivity, and Authority' [1993] University of Pennsylvania Law Review 549

Danziger S, Levav J and Avnaim-Pesso L, 'Extraneous Factors in Judicial Decisions' (2011) 108 Proceedings of the National Academy of Sciences of the United States of America 6889

Del Mar M, 'The Forward-Looking Requirement of Formal Justice: Neil MacCormick on Consequential Reasoning' (2015) 6 Jurisprudence 429

Douglas G, Pearce J and Woodward H, 'Cohabitants, Property and the Law: A Study of Injustice' (2009) 72 Modern Law Review 24

Douzinas C and Gearey A, *Critical Jurisprudence: The Political Philosophy of Justice* (Hart 2005)

Dworkin R, 'Objectivity and Truth: You'd Better Believe It' (1996) 25 Philosophy & Public Affairs 87

_, *Law's Empire* (Hart 1998)

Dyzenhaus D, *Hard Cases in Wicked Legal Systems: Pathologies of Legality* (Oxford University Press 2010)

Eco U, *The Open Work* (Harvard University Press 1989)

Evans N and Levinson SC, 'The Myth of Language Universals: Language Diversity and Its Importance for Cognitive Science' (2009) 32 Behavioral and Brain Sciences 429

Frankenberg G, 'How to Do Projects with Comparative Law - Notes of an Expedition to the Common Core' (2006) 6 Global Jurist Advances

Gazal-Ayal O and Sulitzeanu-Kenan R, 'Let My People Go: Ethnic In-Group Bias in Judicial Decisions—Evidence from a Randomized Natural Experiment' (2010) 7 Journal of Empirical Legal Studies 403

Glenn HP, *Legal Traditions of the World: Sustainable Diversity in Law* (Oxford University Press 2010)

Greenawalt K, *Law and Objectivity* (Oxford University Press, 1995)

Hansen M-BM, 'On the Availability of "literal" Meaning: Evidence from Courtroom Interaction' (2008) 40 Journal of Pragmatics 1392

Hart HLA, 'Positivism and the Separation of Law and Morals' (1958) 71 Harvard Law Review 593

_, *Essays in Jurisprudence and Philosophy* (Oxford University Press 1983)

_, *The Concept of Law* (Penelope Bulloch and Joseph Raz eds, 2nd edition, Oxford University Press 1997)

Kozinski A, 'What I Ate for Breakfast and Other Mysteries of Judicial Decision Making' (1992) 26 Loy. LAL Rev. 993

Kuhn TS, *The Structure of Scientific Revolutions: 50th Anniversary Edition* (University of Chicago Press 2012)

Langacker R, *Foundations of Cognitive Grammar: Volume II: Descriptive Application* (Stanford University Press 1991)

Langacker RW, *Language and Its Structure: Some Fundamental Linguistic Concepts* (Harcourt, Brace & World 1968)

_, *Cognitive Linguistics Research [CLR]: Concept, Image, and Symbol: The Cognitive Basis of Grammar (2)* (De Gruyter Mouton 1990)

_, *Investigations in Cognitive Grammar* (De Gruyter Mouton 2009)

Legrand P, 'European Legal Systems Are Not Converging' (1996) 45 The International and Comparative Law Quarterly 52

_, 'Against a European Civil Code' (1997) 60 The Modern Law Review 44

Leiter B, 'Legal Realism and Legal Positivism Reconsidered*' (2001) 111 Ethics 278

Levinson SC, *Pragmatics* (Cambridge University Press 1983)

MacCormick N, *Legal Reasoning and Legal Theory* (Clarendon Press 1994)

_, 'Reasonableness and Objectivity' (1998) 74 Notre Dame L. Rev. 1575

'Natural Language Toolkit — NLTK 3.0 Documentation' <http://www.nltk.org/> accessed 3 June 2016

Popper K, *The Logic of Scientific Discovery* (Routledge 2005)

Rodriguez-Blanco V, 'Objectivity in Law' (2010) 5 Philosophy Compass 240

Rorty R, *Objectivity, Relativism, and Truth* (Cambridge University Press 1991)

Skoczeń I, 'Minimal Semantics and Legal Interpretation' [2015] International Journal for the Semiotics of Law - First Online: 20 October 2015

Zimmermann R, 'Civil Code and Civil Law - The Europeanization of Private Law within the European Community and the Re-Emergence of a European Legal Science' (1994) 1 Columbia Journal of European Law 63

Zirk-Sadowski M, 'Interpretation of Law and Judges Communities' (2012) 25 International Journal for the Semiotics of Law - 473

Zucca L, *Constitutional Dilemmas: Conflicts of Fundamental Legal Rights in Europe and the USA* (Oxford University Press 2007)

Chapter 1
The Grammar of Bias: Judicial Impartiality in European Legal Systems

1. Introduction

The concept of judicial objectivity is a cornerstone of modern legal systems. This chapter discusses the interplay between the lexical uses of the concept of judicial *objectivity* in cases that review the judicial impartiality of the court. The data for this project was retrieved from a large sample of cases: over a thousand decisions from Brazil, Hungary, Italy, Lithuania, Slovakia, Slovenia, Spain, Romania and the UK. The data analysis shows that in the case of alleged judicial bias, the concept of objectivity is cited to justify different judicial activities such as the assessment of procedures adopted by an allegedly biased court or the existence of subjective interest in a case. In particular, the study provides a strong indication of what Legrand called 'pre-judices', which are the cultural aspects that are embedded in the professional socialisation processes of each legal system.[83]

Legrand's ideas relied on deductive analysis but, from a social perspective, there were too many variables and too little data. This study focuses on lexical reference – retrieved by using Langacker's studies on grammar – to the concept of objectivity in cases in which there is an allegation of judicial bias.[84] The results show substantial differences in how courts in different legal systems engage with objective and personal allegations of bias. An objective allegation of bias suggests that the judge has a direct interest in the issues upon which s/he is called to decide. A personal allegation of bias suggests that a judge might have a personal or professional connection with

83 Pierre Legrand, 'Against a European Civil Code' (1997) 60 The Modern Law Review 44; Sol Azuelos-Atias, 'Semantically Cued Contextual Implicatures in Legal Texts' (2010) 42 Journal of Pragmatics 728.

84 Ronald Langacker, *Foundations of Cognitive Grammar: Volume II: Descriptive Application* (Stanford University Press 1991); Deirdre Wilson and Dan Sperber, 'Relevance Theory' in Laurence R Horn and Gregory L Ward (eds), *The Handbook of Pragmatics* (Blackwell 2006).

one of the parties. In the sample considered in this study, an objective allegation of bias tends to support narratives that justify an analysis of evidence and the facts of the case. Variations in how legal systems deliver decisions strongly support Legrand's ideas of pre-judices.[85]

This chapter is divided into five sections, including an introduction and a conclusion. The introduction explains the project's methodology. The second section provides a theoretical overview of the interplay between the concept of objectivity and the concept of judicial bias. Sections three and four discuss cases of objective and subjective bias. The conclusion reflects on the project's results.

2. Judicial Impartiality

This book discusses how judges qualify the concept of objectivity; in this section I focus on how they describe the relationship between impartiality and judicial objectivity. The existence of a direct connection between judicial objectivity and judicial impartiality is a key element in modern liberal democracy. For instance, there is some overlap in the meanings of objective interpretation and impartiality in Article 6[1] of the European Convention on Human Rights.[86] In this chapter, though, I focus on interpreting data that describes the epistemic use of the concept of objectivity in cases that discuss an allegation of judicial bias across different legal systems. The focus of this analysis is thus to verify the hypothesis of variations in how judges defined the concept of objectivity. This objective required a large sample of cases and a group of researchers with the lexical expertise necessary to extract contextual information from case law material.

The cases considered were appeal cases or first instance rulings over an ancillary issue in which the impartiality of the judge or an expert witness was questioned for one reason or another. When deciding on an ancillary issue or an appeal case, the court has to provide objective narratives that confirm or deny the existence of an improper connection between the court or an expert witness and the object of the dispute. For instance, in the R v Bow Street Metropolitan Stipendiary Magistrate Ex Parte Pinochet Ugarte

85 Legrand (n 1) 51; Azuelos-Atias (n 1) 731.
86 *The European Convention on Human Rights* (1950).

case (hereafter Pinochet n. 2), Lord Hoffmann's impartiality was successfully questioned by the legal team representing the former dictator on the grounds that Lord Hoffmann was an unpaid director of a charity associated with Amnesty International.[87] In Pinochet n. 2, the House of Lords, using the reasonable person as a standard, explained that a perception of bias was sufficient to support a request for a retrial.

This chapter reports on the epistemic methods that courts like the House of Lords (now the UK Supreme Court) adopt to engage with an allegation of bias.[88] The epistemic method, such as the House of Lords' evaluation of a reasonable perception of bias, is retrieved exclusively from a contextual reading of the decision text. This process does not involve a qualitative analysis of the function carried out by the judicial process (e.g. to deliver an objective decision).[89] The study thus does not strive to evaluate the quality of the epistemic method adopted by each legal system considered in this project.

The chapter uses data mined from a larger research project aimed at clarifying how judicial narratives qualify the concept of judicial objectivity.[90] That project involved more than twelve researchers and two coordinators. The individual researchers had the linguistic and legal training necessary to analyse a large sample of random cases. I coordinated the final review of the data and provided one of the reports. Each researcher had to report on a sample of at least 100 cases in which the court explicitly qualified the concept of judicial objectivity. The analysis was carried out in two stages. In the first stage, the researchers were required to classify the type of lexical qualification of the concept of objectivity. This was a quasi-mechanical task that did not require the use of Natural Language Toolkit software.[91]

---

87 *R v Bow Street Metropolitan Stipendiary Magistrate Ex p Pinochet Ugarte (No2) [2000]* (1999) 1 AC 119 (HL).

88 Günter Frankenberg, 'How to Do Projects with Comparative Law - Notes of an Expedition to the Common Core' (2006) 6 Global Jurist Advances.

89 Langacker (n 2); Ronald Langacker, *The Foundations of Cognitive Grammar: Volume I: Theoretical Prerequisites* (Stanford University Press 1999).

90 Vito Breda and Lidia Rodak, 'Introduction' in Vito Breda and Lidia Rodak (eds), *Diverse Narratives of Legal Objectivity: An Interdisciplinary Perspective* (Peter Lang 2016).

91 'Natural Language Toolkit — NLTK 3.0 Documentation' <http://www.nltk.org/> accessed 3 June 2016.

A national legal database provided a list of cases in which a court referred to the concept of objectivity. The investigator ensured that lexical references to judicial objectivity were not a false positive or part of a scrawling verbiage in which the words 'objectivity', 'objectively' or 'objective' carried a limited reference to their broader lexical significance. For instance, epistemic processes that qualify bias were often proposed by a party that alleged the impartiality of a judge, but the courts did not deem such narratives persuasive.

The selected cases were classified according to the object of the decision. This chapter only reports on cases in which there was an allegation of judicial bias, which included judicial narratives (hereafter termed extracts) that indicate a court's intention to qualify the concept of judicial objectivity. These types of narratives were divided into different groups:

a. the court refers to the subjective impartiality of the judge
b. the court refers to the objective impartiality of the judge
c. the court refers to external objective criteria
d. the court refers to the activity of a third party (subjective bias)
e. the court's decision is de facto unbiased
f. the court's decision considers all the facts of the case
g. the court's decision refers to the opinion of experts
h. the court's decision refers to legal rules and procedures

Negative variations, in which the court defines what could not be associated with the concept of objectivity, were considered false positives.

As mentioned in the introduction, the second stage of the study involved a contextual analysis of the extracts with the goal of labelling their cognitive use, as perceived by the researcher. Skoczeń adopts an analogous methodology aimed at distinguishing context from co-text which might project individual perceptions on a semiotic analysis.[92] The effectiveness of Skoczeń's methodology is explained in the introduction and does not need to be fully reproduced in this chapter. However, it is essential to recall that the focus of this part of the study is to show the national contextual aspects that qualify

92 Izabela Skoczeń, 'Minimal Semantics and Legal Interpretation' (2015) International Journal for the Semiotics of Law - <http://link.springer.com/10.1007/s11196-015-9448-3> accessed 6 June 2016.

the concept of objectivity in each legal system under consideration. By contrast, Skoczeń's methodology sought, within the limit of reasonableness, to reduce all possible references to the co-text that might obscure legal practice.[93] She did so by combining Levinson's enumerations of contextual elements and Azuelos-Atias's classification of legal common knowledge.[94] Skoczeń's methodology has the merit of reducing the semantic context in which the concept of truth is defined, for instance, by legal theorists. This reduction was part of her project because it decreased the number of variables without hindering Skoczeń's contention.

How much text can be eliminated without losing significant data or becoming overwhelmed by variables is a crucial issue for any linguistic study.[95] In a large project that analyses different national legal systems, both semantic structures and relevant contexts cannot be rigidly limited. As Levinson points out, comparing cognitive contexts across languages reveals little evidence of convergence;[96] epistemic assumptions over linguistic cognitive processes do not travel well across national borders.

The aim of the project was not, however, to define the concept of judicial objectivity but to provide an indication of the contextual elements that each legal system adopts to define its own concept of objectivity. These contextual narratives are distinctive of a legal system:

> Contextual significances represent some of the key elements of legal interpretation. The most important type of cognitive effect achieved by processing an input in a context is a contextual implication, a conclusion deducible from the input and the context together, but from neither input nor context alone.[97]

Contextual implications are strictly linked to a specific sociological community. They represent, it can thus be reasonably suggested, what Legrand called 'professional pre-judices':

---

93 Skoczeń (n 10) 2.

94 Azuelos-Atias (n 1); Stephen C Levinson, *Pragmatics* (Cambridge University Press 1983) 5; Nicholas Evans and Stephen C Levinson, 'The Myth of Language Universals: Language Diversity and Its Importance for Cognitive Science' (2009) 32 Behavioral and Brain Sciences 429.

95 Levinson (n 12) 5.

96 Evans and Levinson (n 12).

97 Empahsis on the original text. Azuelos-Atias (n 1) 251.

> These pre-judices—I use the term in a purely etymological rather than negative or acquired—sense are actively forged in fundamental social structures such as the educational process, in which law students are immersed and through which they learn the values, beliefs, dispositions, justifications and the practical consciousness that allows them to consolidate a cultural code, to crystallize their identities and to become professionally socialized.[98]

According to Legrand, pre-judices are mildly complex epistemic practices that are part of the professional socialisation processes that distinguish each legal system. By providing the vessel of shared meanings, they facilitate the inner workings of a legal system.[99] Similar conclusions are drawn by Azuelos-Atias.[100]

In some cases in this study, the court decided to *evaluate* the evidence that a judge owned shares in a company involved in a dispute on which s/he was called on to decide. In this case, extracts – a sentence or group of sentences that referred to the concept of objectivity – were part of the court's decision to explain a specific activity that was perceived by the court as a necessary aspect of a fair judicial process. These activities included an evaluation of the allegations, a description of the facts and an analysis of the procedure that was perceived to be affected by bias. In addition, some judicial narratives employed rhetorical or explicative reasoning, in which the extracts provide an indication of a connection between judicial narratives and the concept of objectivity. Their contextual evaluation shows how those narratives are used, in practice, in different legal systems.

The analysis of contextual interpretations indicated that most legal systems included in this study associate the allegation of objective bias with the need to evaluate factual narratives that do not evince significant degrees

---

98 Pierre Legrand, 'European Legal Systems Are Not Converging' (1996) 45 The International and Comparative Law Quarterly 52, 51. For a general analisys of comparative law as an analisys of a cultural artifact, see: Frankenberg (n 6).

99 Legrand (n 1) 51.

100 From the point of view of testing the comprehension procedure, the context's only function is to determine the common ground that includes, as noted, the set of all possible contextual assumptions of the text...the common ground of the legal discourse include all the knowledge based on "ordinary ways of doing things familiar to lawyers in their everyday professional life" – namely, all the knowledge of the legal system and legal procedure familiar to lawyers Azuelos-Atias (n 1) 732.

of national difference. Allegations of subjective bias, by contrast, are associated with a cluster of activities that appear to be based on national variations. For instance, the Slovakian sample shows that compliance with procedural requirements is sufficient to rebut a claim of subjective bias, but in the UK, mere procedural soundness of a process cannot singlehandedly overcome the persuasiveness of an allegation of subjective bias.[101] These types of national variations in judicial practice are very similar to what Legrand considers pre-judices.[102]

The lexical variations in how national systems construct judicial narratives that are all associated, in different contextual manners, with the concept of objectivity, is among the most revealing aspects of this study, and it has a twofold implication: first, the study supports the existence of Legrand's idea of national pre-judices; second, the study results inform large international organisations such as the European Union (EU) or the World Bank of variations in the lexical structure of judicial decisions.[103] Posner, who has a less critical perception of the effect of the convergence of legal systems than Legrand, recommends adapting international legal rules to local cultures.[104] Before I substantiate my claim, several issues have to be addressed as part of a preliminary analysis.

This research is not a comparative study that adopts a functional approach,[105] so it neither assumes nor contests the claim that modern democratic legal systems require similar fundamental characteristics such as ensuring an objective and independent judicial system.[106] Among the functional

101 *R. v Bow Street Metropolitan Stipendiary Magistrate Ex p. Pinochet Ugarte (No. 2) [2000]* (n 5).

102 Legrand (n 1); Legrand (n 16).

103 Legrand (n 16) 51; Richard A Posner, 'Creating a Legal Framework for Economic Development' (1998) 13 The World Bank Research Observer 1, 5–6.

104 Posner (n 9) 6; David W Leebron, 'Claims for Harmonization: A Theoretical Framework' (1996) 27 Canadian Business Law Journal 63; Eckart Brodermann, 'Impact of the UNIDROIT Principles on International Contract and Arbitration Practice: The Experience of a German Lawyer' (2011) 16 Uniform Law Review 589.

105 Esin Orücü, 'Developing Conparative Law' in David Nelken and Esin Orücü (eds), *Comparative Law a Handbook.* (Hart 2007).

106 The Functional Approach is analysed in a plethora of outlets and it has been used in a series of well-reputed studies. See, for instance, these analyses: Mark

requirements of modern civil procedures is regulating how evidence is presented to the court.[107] If the regimes of evidence were too strict, the court would not be able to find a reasonable representation of the truth. There is a rich literature that questions the validity of the functional approach in comparative legal studies,[108] but this study focuses on how legal narratives are extracted from the concept of objectivity to support a distinctive court epistemic practice.[109] Thus, the assumption adopted in the study is that legal objectivity is used as a lexical device by the courts in cases in which it is called upon to explain a judicial narrative. Furthermore, the project's aim is not to assert which legal system might be better or worse at ensuring the functional independence of its judiciary.

As noted above, the project instead reveals a cluster of narratives associated with the concept of judicial objectivity. It was not clear at the outset whether a particular legal system had a distinctive cluster of textual references to the concept of judicial objectivity. Moreover, if each country has a cluster of jurisprudential significances connected to the concept of objectivity, which is one of the research hypotheses, would these clusters be similar or diverging? The answer to the last research question is of particular importance for the judiciaries of EU member states which, over the past thirty years, have been asked to implement EU treaties and Community

---

Tushnet, *Weak Courts, Strong Rights, Judicial Review and Social Welfare Rights in Comparative Constitutional Law* (Princeton University Press 2008); Michele Graziadei, 'Legal Transplants and the Frontiers of Legal Knowledge' (2009) 10 Theoretical Inquiries in Law 723; Peter De Cruz, *Comparative Law in a Changing World* (Routledge-Cavendish 2007) 334; Esin Orücü, 'Comparative Law in Practice' in David Nelken and Esin Orücü (eds), *Comparative Law: A Handbook.* (Hart 2007); Konrad Zweigert, *Introduction to Comparative Law* (Clarendon Press; Oxford University Press 1998) 34.

107 Vito Breda and Matteo Vricella, 'English Pragmatism and Italian Virtue: A Comparative Analysis of the Regime of Illegally Obtained Evidence in Civil Law Proceedings between Italy and England' (2014) 21 Maastricht Journal of European and Comparative Law 428.

108 Rodolfo Sacco, 'Legal Formants: A Dynamic Approach to Comparative Law' (1991) 39 The American Journal of Comparative Law 343; Helena Whalen-Bridge, 'The Reluctant Comparatist: Teaching Common Law Reasoning to Civil Law Students and the Future of Comparative Legal Skills' (2008) 58 Journal of Legal Education; Orücü (n 12).

109 Langacker (n 2).

Law in a uniform manner. Knowing how diverse the lexical understanding of general concepts was across EU judicial systems is also essential for proposed plans such as notion of a constitution for Europe.[110] These types of ambitious plans depend enormously on the existence of a common understanding of general legal concepts. The study shows that, even at the lexical level, all the legal systems considered are semantically distinctive and thus unqualified general terms such as 'judicial objectivity', 'transparency' and 'equality' tend to generate different practical results in different countries. One issue that may require further research is whether significant cross-fertilisation might aid the development of common understandings.

3. Judicial bias: A theoretical overview

Judicial impartiality is an essential element of the rule of law.[111] However, the debate over judicial impartiality is also associated with a multi-faceted debate that questions the conceptual, explanatory and social plausibility of an unbiased judicial system.[112] For instance, Baum questions the plausibility of judicial independence.[113] There are also strongly supported narratives from the critical legal studies movement that have focused on the political nature of judicial power in modern constitutional systems.[114] From Christodoulidis's perspective, any attempt to describe a legal system as impartial inevitably obscures some of its ideological connotations.[115] Some

---

110 Legrand (n 1) 50. V Breda, 'A European Constitution in a Multinational Europe or a Multinational Constitution for Europe?' (2006) 12 European Law Journal 330.

111 E. Voeten, 'The Impartiality of International Judges: Evidence from the European Court of Human Rights' (2008) 102 American Political Science Review 417.

112 Ibidem.

113 L. Baum, 'What Judges Want: Judges' Goals and Judicial Behavior' (1994) 47 Political Research Quarterly 749.

114 Emilios Christodoulidis, 'Constitutional Irresolution: Law and the Framing of Civil Society' (2003) 9 European Law Journal 4001; Christodoulidis (n 18); G. Schubert, 'Political Culture and Judicial Ideology: Some Cross- and Subcultural Comparisons', (1997) 9 Comparative Political Studies 363.

115 This point is developed, in particular, against Dworkin's idea of law as a cognitive process aimed at protecting rights. Christodoulidis, *Law and Reflexive Politics* (n 32).

of these polemics question the very basis of modern liberal democracy, but the large number of cases considered in this project does not confirm that political bias is perceived as relevant, which may be an unexpected outcome to many observers.

A theoretical discussion over the impartiality of judges engages two distinctive areas of law. The first, which has already been cited, is a constitutional requirement for political impartiality. The discussion of constitutional impartiality forms part of the debates between radical democrats and positivists concerning the interplay between liberalism and judicial narratives. Judges are expected to decide cases without allowing their political views to affect their decisions.[116] This is among the best-known functional requirements of the rule of law; however, it is also among the most contested. This debate is much more prominent at the theoretical level than in actual cases; this study, which focuses on judicial narratives, found only two cases in which a court has been asked to respond to claims of ideological bias. In a case discussed by the Budapest Metropolitan Court, No. 27.P. 24.578/2006./3, the judges decided that 'due to the requirement of political and ideological neutrality, it is beyond the court's jurisdiction to take a stance on ideological or political questions'.[117] This lexical engagement might trigger a series of debates, especially in former colonies, over the political nature of courts established by the controlling power to suppress the indigenous and poorer sections of society so as to maintain control by a ruling elite. This debate is particularly vigorous in Australia.[118]

A second example of the requirement for political neutrality in a general sense can be found in the Supreme Court of Lithuania (CLS) case No. 3K-3-93/2011, in which the court investigated the allocation of cases among Lithuanian jurisdictions.[119] These are the only cases in which judges were

116 Gary Slapper, *The English Legal System: 2012–2013* (Routledge 2012) 398.

117 No. 27.P. 24.578/2006./3.

118 Nicholas Pengelley, 'The Hindmarsh Island Bridge Act: Must Laws Based on the Race Power Be for the "Benefit" of Aborigines and Torres Strait Islanders? And What Has Bridge Building Got to Do with the Race Power Anyway?' (1998) 20 Sydney Law Review, The: 144; Robert Dubler, 'Race and the Constitution' (2002) 76 Australian Law Journal 456.

119 No. 3K-3-93/2011.

accused of political bias. The lack of judicial narratives that challenge the political impartiality of judges might suggest the need for a qualitative analysis. It could be argued that the level of doctrinal animosity linked to the debate over judicial impartiality in liberal democracies, such as the one suggested by the CLS,[120] should have resulted in a greater number of challenges to political independence.

An additional area of law related to the debate over judicial impartiality concerns the relevant procedural requirements for trials. The impartiality of the court is questioned because one of the judges has a direct or relational interest in the issue on which the court has been asked to rule. For instance, a judge cannot have a direct monetary interest in an issue on which s/he is asked to decide. A relational interest is less obvious than a direct interest, since the judge's impartiality is questioned because of an incidental connection with an issue on which s/he must rule. Pinochet n. 2 is an excellent example of the potential effects of having a judge who has only a relational interest in a case.[121] There, the House of Lords decided against extraditing the former Chilean head of state to Spain.

The British authorities had arrested Mr Pinochet in response to a Spanish international warrant that alleged he committed a series of human rights violations during his tenure as Chile's head of state. After a series of appeals, the case reached the House of Lords, which initially allowed the UK authorities to complete the extradition procedures. However, after that decision, the legal team representing Mr Pinochet discovered that Lord Hoffman had been the unpaid director of a charity linked to Amnesty International. It was hardly a sinecure and did not involve Amnesty itself, but that organisation had campaigned vigorously against human rights violations in Chile and for the arrest of Mr Pinochet.[122]

There was no indication, the Lords pointed out, that Lord Hoffmann's decision was substantially or procedurally impaired by his role as an

---

120 Christodoulidis, 'Constitutional Irresolution: Law and the Framing of Civil Society' (n 32).

121 *R. v Bow Street Metropolitan Stipendiary Magistrate Ex p. Pinochet Ugarte (No. 2) [2000]* (n 5).

122 William J Aceves, 'Liberalism and International Legal Scholarship: The Pinochet Case and the Move Toward a Universal System of Transnational Law Litigation' (2000) 41 Harvard International Law Journal 129, 166.

unpaid director of the charity. However, the perception that he had a relational interest in the case was sufficient to grant a petition that allowed for Mr Pinochet's retrial. The justification for this decision is of particular interest to the present project, because the Lords showed a concern with objective evidence and the link to perceptions of bias. In this case, the Lords argued that an external observer who had a fair understanding of the relevant facts of the case might have deemed the decision to be based on one judge's personal beliefs:

> The court cannot rely on its knowledge of the integrity of the judge concerned to outweigh the appearance of bias to the eye of the bystander. The reference point must remain the reasonable observer. This is consistent with the test laid down under article 6(1) of the European Convention for the Protection of Human Rights and Fundamental Freedoms. [...] The appropriate test is whether a fair-minded observer with knowledge of the relevant facts would have a suspicion of bias.[123]

In other words, the perception of impropriety from an external standpoint was sufficient to deem Lord Hoffmann's relational interest pernicious for the entire decision.[124] The connection between the public perception of bias and the concept of objectivity is a distinctive element of the cluster of narratives that UK judges assume are related to an independent decision-making process.

The public perception issue is a clear manifestation of a professional pre-judice, and it is a distinctive element that differentiates the British legal system from its continental peers. In contrast, a contextual analysis of the extracts from the Spanish sample of cases shows that subjective allegations of bias can be rebutted by focusing solely on the case's procedural elements. There is no indication that an epistemic activity is selected with the aim of obscuring, as CLS suggested, the ideological effect of liberalism.

This study confirms Coleman and Leiter's classification of the three stages of metaphysical analysis in legal reasoning: strong, modest and minimal metaphysical practices.[125] The evaluation of factual narratives is dominated

123 *R. v Bow Street Metropolitan Stipendiary Magistrate Ex p. Pinochet Ugarte (No. 2) [2000]* (n 5) 122.

124 The Pinochet n. 2 case was not part of the sample considered in this study.

125 Jules L Coleman and Brian Leiter, 'Determinacy, Objectivity, and Authority' [1993] University of Pennsylvania Law Review 549, 561; Azuelos-Atias (n 1) 734.

by strong metaphysical assumptions, a connection that is also present in theological narratives. Coleman and Leiter's idea of strong metaphysical assumptions is part of an eminently *laic episteme* in which the validity of a given act of legal reasoning depends on the requirements of the scientific method. For instance, judges tasked to evaluate a ballistics report, once they accept the procedural soundness of the scientific method that was adopted by the expert witness delivering said report, will consider the report an objective representation of the truth. Thus, there is a strong connection between scientific and legal methods, which is evident in the lexical structures and contextual interpretations of all the legal systems considered in this study.

The connection is weaker when judges interpret a legal text than when they evaluate the facts of a case.[126] Interpreting a legal text is a metaphysical activity that is bounded by precedents and statutory requirements. The interplay between judicial discretion and textual interpretation is an old chestnut of positivism and need not be reproduced here. It is important to note, however, that Hart and Dworkin's long-distance debate is considered the most thorough articulation of the discussions over the limits of judicial interpretation,[127] and that one agreement that emerged from their exchange is that textual interpretation is not a completely undetermined activity. In Coleman and Leiter's terms, it is thus not a 'weak metaphysical activity' that might deliver unprovable results.[128] Judicial interpretation of a legal text is a restrained activity, which Coleman and Leiter defined as metaphysically modest. It is so by way of comparison to the strong scientific method, which is part of judicial decision-making, and the weak interpretative method, which should not be part of judicial practices.

The key result of the allegations of objective judicial bias considered in this study is that a strong metaphysic is normally used to evaluate the veracity of a claim. A modest metaphysic is adopted in cases in which there is an

126 Coleman and Leiter (n 43).

127 HLA Hart, *The Concept of Law* (Clarendon Press 1961) ch 5; Ronald Dworkin, *Taking Rights Seriously* (Harvard University Press 1978) 14–46; HLA Hart, *The Concept of Law* (Penelope Bulloch and Joseph Raz eds, Oxford University Press 1997) 263 postscript.

128 Christodoulidis, *Law and Reflexive Politics* (n 32).

allegation of subjective judicial bias. The analysis of the data also shows that the modest metaphysic is culturally specific, with each legal system adopting a series of culturally specific pre-judices to assess the plausibility of an allegation of subjective bias.

4. Allegations of objective judicial bias: A common legal language across Europe

In this section, I focus on allegations of objective bias, as when a judge has a financial interest in a case. The study shows that court narratives emphasise the analysis of hard evidence and rely exclusively on scientific methodology such as financial forensic techniques to carry out that analysis. The existence of a common lexical engagement and contextual significance with the allegation of objective bias is an indication of the quality of judicial training across legal systems.

Allegations of objective bias can involve both judges and expert witnesses, but allegations against judges are very rare. In our sample, it is far more common to find allegations of objective bias regarding expert witnesses. For instance, a technical report by a forensics specialist might be erroneous in its conclusion, yet it cannot be considered to be tainted by bias for that reason. In decision no. I Ips 500/2008, the Supreme Court of Slovenia rejected a claim of bias made against the report of an expert witness. Referring to European Court of Human Rights' jurisprudence, the court argued that direct measurements and test results could not have been influenced by the activities of the expert witness; it was a case of evidence independent of interest. Another example of obviously Ockhamist reasoning can be found in the Lithuanian cases. A decision by Kaunas Regional Administrative Court[129] explained that one of the general principles of law is the principle of objectivity, according to which no public officer or administrative employee can participate in drafting an administrative document that might affect him or her directly or indirectly. In the case under discussion, the civil servant was not affected by the report and it was therefore considered unbiased.

The Spanish sample of cases also offers a substantial number of instances in which courts explored potential links between objectivity and impartiality.

---

129 2011-03-24 No. II-112-423/2011.

The Spanish legal system includes a regulatory framework that explicitly regulates allegations of bias against public servants and judges.[130] Furthermore, there is, Gordillo explains, a line of jurisprudence in which the Spanish Constitutional Court squarely engages the issue of judges' impartiality. One of the best-known such decisions is No. 26/2007, which was an ancillary issue discussed as part of the Constitutional Court's review of the 2006 Statute of Catalonia Case,[131] in which the court accepted a motion to disqualify Justice Tremps. In 2006, Tremps co-authored a report which was sent to the Spanish Parliament during discussions about reforming the 1979 Statute of Catalonia.[132] That report was considered, among other aspects of the case, sufficient to support an allegation of bias. Gordillo notes that such strict application of the principle of impartiality is not replicated in Spain beyond the jurisprudence of the constitutional court:[133]

> In principle, the grounds for disqualification of constitutional justices are the same as those of ordinary judges. However, the Constitutional Court long ago declared that the application of grounds for disqualification of constitutional justices does not operate unconditionally, but rather that the interpretation and application of those grounds must be carried out in accordance with the specific nature of the constitutional review.[134]

Given the *sui generis* nature of the jurisprudence of the Spanish Constitutional Court, the sample of Spanish cases considered in this project did not dwell on such decisions. The researchers focused on key aspects of

---

130 Ley Orgánica No. 6/1985 1985; Ley Orgánica No. 8/2011 2011; Constitution (Spain) 1978 s 159.5; Luis I Gordillo, 'Challenging Justices, Disqualifying the Constitutional Court' <http://www.thecourt.ca/2007/12/challenging-justices-disqualifying-the-constitutional-court/> accessed 11 June 2016.

131 Josep Mª Castellà Andreu, *La Sentencia Del Tribunal Constitucional 31/2010, Sobre El Estatuto de Autonomía de Cataluña Y Su Significado Para El Futuro Del Estado Autonómico* (Fundación Ciudadanía y Valores 2010) <http://www.funciva.org/uploads/ficheros_documentos/1284366523_sentencia_del_tc._josep_maria_castella.pdf> accessed 4 December 2015; Ley Orgánica 6/2006, de 19 de julio, de reforma del Estatuto de Autonomía de Cataluña, 2006.

132 Andreu (n 52); Ley Orgánica 6/2006, de 19 de julio, de reforma del Estatuto de Autonomía de Cataluña. (n 52); Ley Orgánica 4/1979, de 18 de diciembre, Estatuto de Autonomía de Cataluña. 1979.

133 Gordillo (n 51).

134 Gordillo (n 51).

the judicial qualifications of allegations of judicial bias in lower courts.[135] In these decisions, courts confirmed that public servants and their actions were to be considered objective because their selection process is impartial and because they are experts in the areas in which they provide evidence.[136]

An allegation of bias in expert witness statements was engaged by the Budapest Regional Court of Appeal.[137] The court said: 'the witness does not have any financial ties with the plaintiff [...] and does not have any interest in the plaintiff's winning the case. In relation to the case, the witness's status is entirely neutral'.[138] The similarity between the narratives derived from the Budapest Regional Court's decision and the Spanish cases reported in this project might be unexpected. However, there are actually strong similarities in the epistemic narratives that follow an allegation of objective bias among all the judicial systems considered in this project.

The specific reasons for such similarities would require a qualitative analysis that includes semi-structured interviews with judges, but there is strong enough evidence from a purely lexical analysis of the cases to suggest a relationship between metaphysical positivism, which holds that only allegations proved by evidence can be considered scientifically truthful, and legal positivism. Evidence has to be based on factual narratives or provided by professional or academic experts.[139] This result confirms Coleman and Leiter's classification of three types of metaphysical analysis in legal reasoning. In particular, the study shows that allegations of objective bias are assessed by adopting hard metaphysical narratives which focus on evidence and the scientific method.

---

135 Ley Orgánica No. 6/1985 (n 51).

136 STS 01/II/11, STS 03/II/11; STS 09/II/11; STS 11/V/10; STS 13/V/11, STS 24/V/11.

137 No. 14.Gf.40.401/2011/4 (FIT-H-GJ-2012-57).

138 No. 14.Gf.40.401/2011/4 (FIT-H-GJ-2012-57).

139 Jules L Coleman and Brian Leiter, 'Determinacy, Objectivity, and Authority' [1993] 142 University of Pennsylvania Law Review 549, 559.

5. Subjective judicial bias: The national grammar of judicial bias

In the previous section, I discussed the narratives that courts associate with allegations of objective bias. I explained that all legal systems considered in this project focus on hard evidence in such matters. While many might have expected this outcome, at the outset of this research, there were doubts over the quality of the decision-making process in patrimonial political systems such as Italy's. Fukayama uses the term 'low trust equilibrium' to define the interplay between Italian citizens and public institutions.[140] However, the textual analysis of subjective allegations of judicial bias has led to one of the most interesting results of this project: allegations of subjective judicial bias can be a proxy for a large variation in narratives and related epistemic activities. These variations in the narratives are the manifestation in lexical terms of Legrand's pre-judices.[141] Pre-judices are often encumbered contextual elements that legal practitioners perceive as the epistemic requirements of a good decision and, in common law countries, as good law.[142] For instance, Azuelos-Atias discusses the judicial qualification of a 'personal threat' (as described by section 192 of the Israeli Penal Code) in Israeli jurisprudence,[143] which over the years has inserted the reasonable person as one criterion for evaluating the subjective fear induced by a personal threat.[144] Azuelos-Atias shows that, by considering the reasonable person as one evaluation factor, courts normally provide decisions that are more predictable than judgments that focus only on the semantic of section 192.[145] The increase in predictability brought about by contextual references, as in the reasonable person in the case considered by Azuelos-Atias, might not meet the requirements of hard metaphysic,[146] yet it does gives an indication of a distinctive Israeli pre-judice

140 Francis Fukuyama, *Political Order and Political Decay: From the Industrial Revolution to the Globalisation of Democracy* (Profile Books 2014) 7; 16.

141 Legrand (n 1) 51.

142 Jan Komárek, 'Reasoning with Previous Decisions: Beyond the Doctrine of Precedent' (2013) 61 American Journal of Comparative Law 149.

143 Law No. 5737/1977, Penal Law 1977.

144 Azuelos-Atias (n 1) 737.

145 Azuelos-Atias (n 1) 741; Wilson and Sperber (n 2).

146 Coleman and Leiter (n 43); Karl Popper, *The Logic of Scientific Discovery* (Routledge 2005) 17.

in evaluating personal threat allegations. Contextual legal discourse restricts, as is expected in any interpretative activity, the possible textual significance. This conclusion is very similar to the one proposed in Leiter and Coleman's idea of modest objectivity.[147] One of the problems with Azuelos-Atias's narrative and with Legrand's article is that there are too many variables and not enough cases. This study is one of the few to retrieve evidence of national case clusters in a large-scale comparative analysis.

In the last chapter of this book, I provide an analysis of the matrix formed by the extracts and contextual assumptions that emerge from that large-scale analysis. Table 1 shows the complexity and articulation of judicial qualifications of the concept of objectivity. In this part, I focus particularly on those instances that demonstrate the range of national judicial epistemic practices generated by allegations of subjective bias. If a nation's legal community views an allegation of judicial subjective bias as improperly dealt with, that perception tends to have a ripple effect across the entire legal system. The Italian judicial establishment has taken a long time to recover from the effects of improperly handling cases of allegations of subjective judicial bias in which one of the parties was associated with the Sicilian Mafia.[148] Corrado Carnevale, the former president of the Italian Supreme Court of Cassation, was accused of having an indirect personal relationship with an Italian crime syndicate, through a series of Sicilian politicians. Politicians in Italy act as kingpins of a network of clienteles,[149] which in southern Italy are often though by no means always involved with organised crime. The term clientelism is used to define the 'informal network of power relations between individuals' which distinguishes Italian politics.[150] The practice of clientelism originated in rural societies and included an informal vertical power relation between the power holder such as the patron or landowner and a number of inferiors like seasonal workers. However, the new Italian clientelism is horizontal and

---

147 Coleman and Leiter (n 43).

148 Raffaello Magi, 'Come si impermeabilizza la camera di consiglio. Brevi note sul caso Carnevale' [2003] Questione Giustizia.

149 Fukuyama (n 61) 7;16; Vito Breda, 'How to Reverse the Italian Brain Drain: A Master Class from Australia' (2014) 52 International Migration 64; Mario Caciagli, 'The Long Life of Clientelism in Southern Italy' in Jun'ichi Kawata (ed), *Comparing political corruption and clientelism* (Ashgate 2006) 158.

150 Caciagli (n 70) 158.

might include a nationwide network of individuals that exchange tangible favours like jobs, public contracts, and political support at a nationwide level.[151] In cases of allegations of judicial subjective bias, clientelism is difficult to prove. By contrast, nepotism, in which members of a family receive undue benefits, is relatively easy to prove by the existence of familial relation. However, it is very difficult to present evidence of subjective bias when there is no direct personal connection between a judge and the party. The judge might have a strong personal connection with powerful members of the clientele. A case in which the judge is part of a panel might involve the interest of another member of the clientele but the relationship between the judge and the person affected is highly informal and exceedingly indirect.

The context of the effect of Italian organised crime on that nation's institutions is distinctive, but it is still important for all legal systems to project a complete lack of personal bias. For instance, in cases discussing an allegation of subjective judicial bias, Hungarian and Slovakian judges tend to focus on the procedural correctness of decisions in which a party alleges an effect of bias. This approach might be perceived as a way to deflect, rather than investigate and confirm or refute, allegations of subjective bias. It could be argued, as the Slovakian researcher pointed out in her final report, that by focusing on the procedural appropriateness of the judicial decision, the allegation of judicial subjective bias remains unaddressed. This aspect of the project requires further investigation, but it is important at this stage to remember that the epistemic activities associated with the qualification of the concept of judicial objectivity should be perceived by a national community of legal professionals as adequate. In Slovakia, focusing on the procedural appropriateness of a decision is sufficient to reject an allegation of subjective bias. Analogously in Italy, a lack of *direct* personal connection with an individual involved in organised crime is sufficient to repel allegations of bias.

An example of judicial reasoning derived from the concept of objectivity appears in the Slovenian Supreme Court's Decision No. I R 13/2010. One party was a judge at the same tribunal in which the case had been heard, while one of the respondents was the judge's husband.[152] These circumstances provided evidence to sustain the appellant's claim of subjective judicial bias.

151 Caciagli (n 70) 158.
152 No. I R 13/2010.

Similar narratives can be extracted from cases of the Supreme Court of the Slovak Republic.[153] In case III. ÚS 347/08, a judge and one of the legal counsellors for the plaintiff shared the same residence and contact details. Again, the perception of an improper relationship was considered sufficient by the Slovakian courts to support a claim of judicial bias. However, the allegation of subjective bias, Berdisová' explains, has to be proved by factual evidence.[154] In chapter 4, I discuss the overlap between epistemic methods that combine objective and subjective evaluations, but it is always expected that an allegation of bias be underpinned by evidence. Some legal systems like Italy's might focus on the procedural aspect of the case and may not consider the evidence of a personal relationship with one of the parties as a key aspect of the case, while another, as in the UK, might focus squarely on the perception of a reasonable person. From the Slovakian report, it is reasonably clear that an allegation of subjective bias requires the support of both objective and subjective epistemic practices.

The jurisprudence of the Slovenian Supreme Court also focuses on the procedural effects that a professional relationship might have on the decision of a case. In decision n. I R 138/2009, the court refused a request to transfer a case to a different court, explaining that the mere existence of prior professional contacts between the judge and a party had to be associated with evidence of objective bias.[155] Kristan and Štajnpihler, in their analysis of the Slovenian sample, note:

> Objectivity in the sense of neutrality/impartiality appeared both in civil and public law cases, although it was far more frequently used in civil than criminal law.... All the examples of objectivity in our sample... are tied exclusively to procedural law.

The review of judicial subjective bias in the Slovenian sample is not completely absent, but both Kristan and Štajnpihler agree that courts tend to

---

153 I. ÚS 352/2010, I. ÚS 131/2010, I. ÚS 46/05, II. ÚS 215/2011, II. ÚS 260/2010, II. ÚS 315/2011, III. ÚS 1/2010, III. ÚS 24/05, III. ÚS 36/2011, III. ÚS 47/05, III. ÚS 74/2011, III. ÚS 105/2011, III. ÚS 110/07, III. ÚS 158/08, III. ÚS 257/2011, III. ÚS 347/08, IV. ÚS 23/2011, IV. ÚS 303/2010, IV. ÚS 325/08.

154 Investigators reports are available at 'Australia's Academic and Research Network' <https://www.aarnet.edu.au>.

155 No. I R 138/2009.

focus on compliance with formal criteria of procedural justice rather than evaluating the existence of harmful relationships involving a judge.

A highly articulate analysis of the role of subjective bias appears in the Supreme Court of Lithuania case 2011-03-15 No. 3K-3-110/2011,[156] which explains in detail the process that the parties should expect after an allegation of subjective bias. According to the court, there are two aspects to the requirement of judicial impartiality: one subjective and the other factual. The subjective element of impartiality demands that a judge cannot have any personal prejudices. The objective aspect of impartiality requires that a judge should not have a personal or professional connection with the parties in a legal dispute. In particular, there should not be evidence that casts a *reasonable* doubt on the impartiality of the judge. These are, in Coleman and Leiter's terms, the ideal epistemic conditions.[157]

For instance, the Supreme Court of Lithuania in decision No. 3K-3-110/2011 2011-03-15 explained that a previous professional relationship between one party and a judge does not automatically imply a violation of the principle of impartiality.[158] The test of reasonableness, the Supreme Court of Lithuania pointed out, demands an evaluation of the nature and duration of such a professional relationship and considering any specific circumstances that might impair the independence of the judicial process. The level of articulation of the case No. 3K-3-110/2011 is of particular interest for our discussion because it provides a clear and precise description of the Lithuanian judges' distinctive epistemic activities.

I could continue to provide examples, but it is reasonably clear that allegations of subjective bias tend to be assessed differently than allegations of objective judicial bias across legal systems. In each nation's sample, allegations of subjective bias have been the proxy for a cluster of activities. This cluster is distinctive and, we can reasonably assume, a direct lexical manifestation of Legrand's idea of legal pre-judices as the defining aspect of institutional culture.[159] The cluster also supports Coleman and Leiter's

156 Kazanavičiūtė (n 48).
157 Coleman and Leiter (n 43).
158 2011-03-15 No. 3K-3-110/2011.
159 Legrand (n 1) 51; Fukuyama (n 61) 180.

definition of modest judicial objectivity.[160] Courts develop a constrained set of epistemic methods that is perceived, by the professional community that has chosen it, as objective.

6. Conclusion: The grammar of subjective and objective bias

This chapter has discussed the interplay between the concept of objectivity and judicial impartiality by considering a large sample of cases. It focused on the lexical qualification of the concept of judicial objectivity in relation to an allegation of judicial bias. A graphical representation of the project can be found in Table 1 at the end of this book. Chapter 4 includes an analysis of the visual representation of the matrix of contextual significances formed by the intersection of the extracts and their cognitive uses. The analysis of a large sample of cases considered in this project reveals the existence of two large groups of contextual narratives that each national legal system adopts in cases aimed at qualifying the concept of judicial objectivity. The two groups are related to allegations of objective and subjective bias. In the vast majority of cases, allegations of objective bias trigger an evaluation of factual narratives. This confirmed some of Leiter and Coleman's assumptions on the nature of the relative indeterminacy of judicial practices: modern legal systems combine hard scientific narratives and textual interpretations. An allegation of objective bias leads a court to evaluate hard evidence which has, due to the nature of the scientific method, a limited indeterminacy. The questioning of expert witnesses is also a proxy for analogous judicial qualifications in all the legal systems considered in this project. The sharing of very similar cognitive methods challenges the widely held view that each language adopts a different range of cognitive structures in cases of objective bias, which is one of the suggestions made in Evan and Levinson's article 'The Myth of Language Universals: Language Diversity and its Importance for Cognitive Science'.[161] This is, I have argued in this chapter, turns out not to be the case in today's jurisprudence in European countries. In the case of allegations of objective judicial bias, reliance on the classical manifestations of cognitive methods is a manifestation of

160 Coleman and Leiter (n 43).
161 Evans and Levinson (n 12).

a confidence in scientific methodology.[162] The scientific method applied to judicial reasoning includes the observation of factual events, a dimensional analysis, and an evaluation of the hypotheses that might explain such an event. This coincides with Coleman and Leiter's idea of hard metaphysical reasoning in law.[163]

The second group of narratives is, by contrast, aimed at qualifying a claim of subjective bias. In this case, the concept of judicial objectivity supports larger clusters of contextual activities. Each legal system adopts a group of characteristic epistemic methods to evaluate a claim of subjective bias. In the UK, for instance, a reasonable perception of subjective judicial bias might be sufficient to grant a retrial, while Slovenia might require such a perception to be coupled with a procedural violation. In Lithuania, a judge has to evaluate the specifics of a relationship—its nature, duration, and effects—that might impact a judge's impartiality. These results confirm the assumption of Legrand's pre-judices. In each legal system, the judges are part of professional social groups with distinctive narratives and conceptions of what is right and appropriate. These conceptions are manifested directly in the lexical structure of judicial decisions over allegations of bias. They also indirectly confirm Coleman and Leiter's idea of modest metaphysical reasoning in law. Judges are expected to combine the results of the aforementioned hard metaphysical reasoning with the textual interpretation of a legal text. This interpretative activity is constrained by precedents, even in civil law systems, and by statutory requirements.

Bibliography

Aceves WJ, 'Liberalism and International Legal Scholarship: The Pinochet Case and the Move Toward a Universal System of Transnational Law Litigation' (2000) 41 Harvard International Law Journal, 129

Andreu JMC, *La Sentencia Del Tribunal Constitucional 31/2010, Sobre El Estatuto de Autonomía de Cataluña Y Su Significado Para El Futuro Del Estado Autonómico* (Fundación Ciudadanía y Valores 2010) <http://

162 Thomas S Kuhn, *The Structure of Scientific Revolutions:* (University of Chicago Press 2012); Coleman and Leiter (n 43).

163 Coleman and Leiter (n 43).

www.funciva.org/uploads/ficheros_documentos/1284366523_sentencia_del_tc._josep_maria_castella.pdf> accessed 4 December 2015

Aramburo M and Alonso Agüero San Juan AASJ, 'Spain: Objectivity in Legal Discourse' <https://eprints.usq.edu.au/> accessed 11 June 2016

Azuelos-Atias S, 'Semantically Cued Contextual Implicatures in Legal Texts' (2010) 42 Journal of Pragmatics 728

Baum L, 'What Judges Want: Judges' Goals and Judicial Behavior' (1994) 47 Political Research Quarterly 749

Berdisová L, 'Slovakia: Objectivity in Legal Discourse' 'Australia's Academic and Research Network' <https://www.aarnet.edu.au>

Breda V, 'A European Constitution in a Multinational Europe or a Multinational Constitution for Europe?' (2006) 12 European Law Journal 330

Breda V, 'How to Reverse the Italian Brain Drain: A Master Class from Australia' (2014) 52 International Migration 64

Breda V and Rodak L, 'Introduction' in Vito Breda and Lidia Rodak (eds), *Diverse narratives of legal objectivity: an interdisciplinary perspective* (Peter Lang 2016)

Breda V and Vricella M, 'English Pragmatism and Italian Virtue: A Comparative Analysis of the Regime of Illegally Obtained Evidence in Civil Law Proceedings between Italy and England' (2014) 21 Maastricht Journal of European and Comparative Law 428

Brodermann E, 'Impact of the UNIDROIT Principles on International Contract and Arbitration Practice-The Experience of a German Lawyer' (2011) 16 Uniform Law Review. 589

Caciagli M, 'The Long Life of Clientelism in Southern Italy' in Jun'ichi Kawata (ed), *Comparing political corruption and clientelism* (Ashgate 2006)

Christodoulidis E, *Law and Reflexive Politics* (Kluwer 1998)

_, 'Constitutional Irresolution: Law and the Framing of Civil Society' (2003) 9 European Law Journal 4001

Coleman JL and Leiter B, 'Determinacy, Objectivity, and Authority' [1993] University of Pennsylvania Law Review 549

De Cruz P, *Comparative Law in a Changing World* (Routledge-Cavendish 2007)

Dubler R, 'Race and the Constitution' (2002) 76 Australian Law Journal 456

Dworkin R, *Taking Rights Seriously* (Harvard University Press 1978)

Evans N and Levinson SC, 'The Myth of Language Universals: Language Diversity and Its Importance for Cognitive Science' (2009) 32 Behavioral and Brain Sciences 429

Frankenberg G, 'How to Do Projects with Comparative Law - Notes of an Expedition to the Common Core' (2006) 6 Global Jurist Advances

Fukuyama F, *Political Order and Political Decay: From the Industrial Revolution to the Globalisation of Democracy* (Profile Books 2014)

Gordillo LI, 'Challenging Justices, Disqualifying the Constitutional Court' <http://www.thecourt.ca/2007/12/challenging-justices-disqualifying-the-constitutional-court/> accessed 11 June 2016

Graziadei M, 'Legal Transplants and the Frontiers of Legal Knowledge' (2009) 10 Theoretical Inquiries in Law 723

Hart HLA, *The Concept of Law* (Clarendon Press 1961)

_, *The Concept of Law* (Penelope Bulloch and Joseph Raz eds, Oxford University Press 1997)

Kazanavičiūtė R, 'Lithuania: Objectivity in Legal Discourse' 'Australia's Academic and Research Network' <https://www.aarnet.edu.au>

Komárek J, 'Reasoning with Previous Decisions: Beyond the Doctrine of Precedent' (2013) 61 American Journal of Comparative Law 149

Kuhn TS, *The Structure of Scientific Revolutions:* (University of Chicago Press 2012)

Langacker R, *Foundations of Cognitive Grammar: Volume II: Descriptive Application* (Stanford University Press 1991)

_, *The Foundations of Cognitive Grammar: Volume I: Theoretical Prerequisites* (Stanford University Press 1999)

Leebron DW, 'Claims for Harmonization: A Theoretical Framework' (1996) 27 Canadian Business Law Journal 63

Legrand P, 'European Legal Systems Are Not Converging' (1996) 45 The International and Comparative Law Quarterly 52

_, 'Against a European Civil Code' (1997) 60 The Modern Law Review 44

Levine A, *Economic Morality and Jewish Law* (Oxford University Press 2012)

Levinson SC, *Pragmatics* (Cambridge University Press 1983)

Magi R, 'Come si impermeabilizza la camera di consiglio. Brevi note sul caso Carnevale' [2003] Questione Giustizia

'Natural Language Toolkit — NLTK 3.0 Documentation' <http://www.nltk.org/> accessed 3 June 2016

Orücü E, 'Comparative Law in Practice' in David Nelken and Esin Orücü (eds), *Comparative Law a Handbook.* (Hart 2007)

Pengelley N, 'The Hindmarsh Island Bridge Act: Must Laws Based on the Race Power Be for the "Benefit" of Aborigines and Torres Strait Islanders? And What Has Bridge Building Got to Do with the Race Power Anyway?' (1998) 20 Sydney Law Review, The: 144

Popper K, *The Logic of Scientific Discovery* (Routledge 2005)

Posner RA, 'Creating a Legal Framework for Economic Development' (1998) 13 The World Bank Research Observer 1

Sacco R, 'Legal Formants: A Dynamic Approach to Comparative Law' (1991) 39 The American Journal of Comparative Law 343

Schubert G, 'Political Culture and Judicial Ideology Some Cross-and Subcultural Comparisons' (1977) 9 Comparative Political Studies 363

Skoczeń I, 'Minimal Semantics and Legal Interpretation' [2015] International Journal for the Semiotics of Law - <http://link.springer.com/10.1007/s11196-015-9448-3> accessed 6 June 2016

Slapper G, *The English Legal System: 2012–2013* (13 edition, Routledge 2012)

The European Convention on Human Rights (1950)

Tushnet M, *Weak Courts, Strong Rights Judicial Review and Social Welfare Rights in Comparative Constitutional Law* (Princeton University Press 2008)

Voeten E, 'The Impartiality of International Judges: Evidence from the European Court of Human Rights' (2008) 102 American Political Science Review 417

Whalen-Bridge H, 'The Reluctant Comparatist: Teaching Common Law Reasoning to Civil Law Students to Civil Law Students an the Future of Comparative Legal Skills' (2008) 58 Journal of Legal Education

Wilson D and Sperber D, 'Relevance Theory' in Laurence R Horn and Gregory L Ward (eds), *The handbook of pragmatics* (Blackwell 2006)

Zweigert K, *Introduction to Comparative Law* (Clarendon Press; Oxford University Press 1998)

Chapter 2

Truth and justice as qualifiers of the concept of judicial objectivity

1. Introduction

This chapter discusses the use of terms such as *justice* and *truth* as qualifiers of the concept of objectivity in the judicial discourse. Saul of Tarsus, in Philippians 4.8, makes a direct connection between truth and justice. A Talmudic legal scholar identifies the lies of witnesses as the *geneivat da'at*: the theft of someone's mind.[164] The two qualifiers have different meanings, but given the penury of relevant uses reported in our sample of cases, they will be considered as two distinctive parts of a single chapter. Knowledge, and truth as a logical corollary, is one of Finnis's virtues;[165] in judicial discourse, truth, however, is mostly associated with procedural justice. So, truth is, in judicial discourse, a representation of the facts of the case based on a choreographed presentation of evidence. There are, however, substantial differences in different national legal systems. In England, for instance, there is a procedural assumption of validity for all evidence, even if it has been illegally obtained, that contributes to a truthful representation of the facts.[166] In civil law systems, such as the Italian system, only legitimately obtained documents can be considered by the court.[167] Again, the results support Legrand's idea of national pre-judices.[168]

---

164 Aaron Levine, *Economic Morality and Jewish Law* (Oxford University Press 2012) 33.

165 John Finnis, *Natural Law and Natural Rights* (Oxford University Press 2011) 87.

166 Adrian Keane, *The Modern Law of Evidence* (Oxford University Press 2008).

167 Vito Breda and Matteo Vricella, 'English Pragmatism and Italian Virtue: A Comparative Analysis of the Regime of Illegally Obtained Evidence in Civil Law Proceedings between Italy and England' (2014) 21 Maastricht journal of European and comparative law 428.

168 Pierre Legrand, 'Against a European Civil Code' (1997) 60 The Modern Law Review 44, 50–51.

The correlation between *justice* and objectivity, instead, is often used as *fairness*.[169] This part of the analyses retrieved three distinctive uses. The first group of judicial narratives focused on procedural justice (e.g. a public administration has followed the correct procedures).[170] The second group of significances considered justice as an equitable solution to a dispute (e.g. divorcees should have a fair allocation of their previously shared income).[171] The last group of judicial narratives seeks the allocation of public resources that objectively cover for a need in society.[172] The widespread use of fairness and justice as synonymous is particularly interesting because the coupling of the terms *justice* and *fairness* has been a relatively new phenomenon in legal theory; it is reasonable to assume that it started in 1971 in Rawls's Theory of Justice, and it is normally associated with theories of distributive justice.[173]

This chapter is divided into five sections, including an introduction as the first section and a final concluding section. The second section focuses on the use of objective *truth* as a teleological element in legal theory. The third section discusses the difference between procedural and substantial truth. The fourth discusses the results of this study. The fifth part of the chapter provides a conceptual analysis of the concepts of justice and fairness. The sixth section provides an analysis of the data from the correlation between judicial objectivity and justice.

---

169 John Rawls, 'Justice as Fairness: Political Not Metaphysical', Philosophy and Public Affairs, 14 (3), Summer, 223-51 (1998) 97 International Library of Critical Writings in Economics 250.

170 Victor Tadros, 'Enabling Proceduralism' in Emilios A Christodoulidis and Stephen Tierney (eds), *Public Law and Politics: the scope and limits of constitutionalism* (Ashgate 2008).

171 Heather Lynn Capell, 'After the Glass Has Shattered: A Comparative Analysis of Orthodox Jewish Divorce in the United States and Israel' (1998) 33 Texas International Law Journal 331.

172 D Wincott, 'Reshaping Public Space? Devolution and Policy Change in British Early Childhood Education and Care' (2005) 15 Regional and Federal Studies 453.

173 John Rawls, 'The Idea of Public Reason' in William Rehg (ed), *Deliberative Democracy: Essays on Reason and Politics* (MIT 1997); John Rawls, *Political Liberalism* / (Columbia University Press, 2005).

2. The judicial objective truth, and nothing but the procedural truth

The research shows that truth in judicial discourse is normally associated with procedural elements of the trial. From this perspective, the analysis of truth could be distinguished from a deontological evaluation regarding the role of knowledge in law[174] and the evaluation of factual narratives. There is a degree of overlap between the two, but the activity of evaluating the veracity and the admissibility of evidence is manifested in different narratives. In this part of the book, I will discuss how judges qualify a truthful representation of the events that triggered the legal proceedings. This analysis focused on a small number of instances which account for less than 5% of the cases in which judges provided a qualification of the concept of objectivity. The results are, however, worthy of evaluation since a heuristic analysis of our sample provides strong evidence of national dichotomies surrounding the concept of objectivity, which I describe in other parts of this book.[175] The evidence of Legrand's national pre-judices is perhaps more evident in the category of truth as a qualifier of judicial objectivity.

For instance, in some judicial systems, such as the Italian one, truth is perceived as a procedural aspect of the trial. Taruffo, one of the leading experts in Italian civil procedures, speaks openly of the fear of truth that permeates the Italian judicial system. He called it *verophobia* and he described it as one of the key elements of Italian judicial civil proceedings.[176] The term, which Michele Taruffo takes from Goldman's *Knowledge in a Social World*, suggests that a large section of Italian doctrine (and of the judiciary) mechanically upholds deontological principles that hinder the functioning of the civil justice system.[177] Indeed, the sample of cases from Italy did not yield a single instance in which the court associated truth with objectivity.

---

174 Finnis (n 2) 87.

175 Legrand (n 5); Pierre Legrand, 'European Legal Systems Are Not Converging' (1996) 45 The International and Comparative Law Quarterly 52.

176 Michele Taruffo, 'La Verità Nel Processo' (2012) Rivista Trimestrale di Diritto e Procedura Civile 1117.

177 Alvin I Goldman, *Knowledge in a Social World* (Clarendon Press 1999).

Other legal systems, such as the Slovakian[178] and Slovenian[179] systems, have a series of cases in which truth is coupled with the concept of objectivity. The textual analysis of the sample cases based on Langacker's study on semiotics found these five types of textual references.[180] As discussed in the previous chapter, these cases included judicial narratives (hereafter, the extracts) that indicate a court's intention to qualify the concept of judicial objectivity. These types of narratives were divided into different groups:

The court asserts that its analysis is objectively truthful because:

a. the court refers to facts;
b. the court refers to expert witnesses;
c. the court refers to a truthful interpretation of a legal text;
d. the parties agree on the issue; or
e. it is procedurally accurate.

These are extracted narratives from the texts of the judicial decisions that were evaluated for their functional significance. A similar study has been carried out by, for instance, Skoczeń, in relation to Polish jurisprudential decisions.[181] As mentioned in Chapter One, Skoczeń's analysis allows researchers to focus on the cognitive function that judges associated, in the text, with concepts such as *truth* or a combination of concepts such as *truth and judicial objectivity*.[182] Again, the analysis of the matrix of combinations of truth and justice suggests the existence of unique national clusters of extracts and cognitive usage.[183]

Before I explain the results of the study, a series of issues has to be dealt with as a preliminary debate. Firstly, the study did not evaluate the theoretical possibility that the courts acted under ideal cognitive conditions and would therefore have had all the relevant information related to the cases under

---

178 SR no. PL. ÚS 7/2011, PL. ÚS 9/2007, PL. ÚS 65/2011.
179 Decision No. Kp 2/2009, Decision No. II Ips 423/2008.
180 Ronald Langacker, *Foundations of Cognitive Grammar: Volume II: Descriptive Application* (Stanford University Press 1991).
181 Izabela Skoczeń, 'Minimal Semantics and Legal Interpretation' [2015] International Journal for the Semiotics of Law - 2.
182 Skoczeń (n 18); Sol Azuelos-Atias, 'Semantically Cued Contextual Implicatures in Legal Texts' (2010) 42 Journal of Pragmatics 728.
183 Legrand (n 12).

consideration. In other words, the study did not aim to show the difference between what I might call truth with a capital [T] and the axiomatic limitations associated with the judicial reconstruction of past events. The interplay between [T]ruth and judicial truth is discussed in Coleman and Leiter's idea of modest objectivity in law.[184] The relation between capital [T] truth and judicial truth is also explained in a compelling narrative by Richard Uviller: 'Few would dispute Judge Frankel's theorem that Truth often suffers in the courtroom. He rightly reminds us that in those relatively few cases (civil or criminal) that go to trial, one side or the other seeks – wittingly or unwittingly – to defeat Truth.'[185] Judicial narratives are, in other words, not concerned with Truth with a capital [T]. They are, instead, based on a reasonable representation of past events that the parties and the judge consider relevant for the decision of the case. Judicial truth is, therefore, a small [t] truth that is conceptually similar to Coleman and Leiter's idea of modest objectivity in law.[186] It is noteworthy that the concept of a judicial truth with a small [t] is not antithetical to Coleman And Leiter idea of modest objectivity, which I discuss in other chapters.[187] Uviller's description, however, provides an analysis that is directed to the procedural aspects of the interplay between truth and objectivity, whereas Coleman seeks to disentangle the ontological from the teleological elements of the judicial process. Our study shows that, in the judicial discourse, the search for legally relevant and legally admissible *truth* is mainly dependent on court procedures and the regulatory framework for law professionals.[188] For instance, the admissibility of illicitly obtained evidence is dependent on the judicial recognition of its validity and also on a system of rules that exonerates legal councils from the criminal and civil responsibilities associated with it.

---

184 Jules L Coleman and Brian Leiter, 'Determinacy, Objectivity, and Authority' [1993] University of Pennsylvania Law Review 549.

185 Richard Uviller, 'Advocate, the Truth, and Judicial Hackles: A Reaction to Judge Frankel's Idea' (1975) 123 University of Pennsylvania Law Review 1067, 1069.

186 Coleman and Leiter (n 21).

187 Coleman and Leiter (n 21).

188 Robert Alexy, Ruth Adler and Neil MacCormick, *A Theory of Legal Argumentation: The Theory of Rational Discourse as Theory of Legal Justification* (Oxford University Press 2009).

Secondly, the judicial search for truth is normally limited by judicial procedures and ethical regulations. Lawyers cannot be directly involved in any illegitimate activity that might help the court to discover the truth without incurring professional sanctions. The limit of judicial narratives as an epistemic method to retrieve the truth, instead, has been part of the stable criticism of legal positivism. In the first half of the last century, for instance, the plausibility of trials as fact-finding activities was heavily criticized by the legal realism movement.[189] Perhaps the most recognised contributor to such a criticism is Jerome Frank. Frank's argument is, in short, that facts are so heavily dependent on judicial procedures that, in turn, they might be considered of little relevance in the decision of the case.[190] This point is also developed in Foucault and his conclusion supports a radical critique of institutional power coupled with a nihilist idea of justice: 'Each society has its regime of truth, its general politics of truth.'[191] Truth might be a virtue in Finnis's mind, but realist analyses suggest that, in judicial practices, 'truth' is the domain of the Panglosses.[192]

Rorty has recently revisited some of the critiques made against social science's epistemic methods and provided a less militant analysis.[193] It is, however, relevant to this chapter to discuss the functional uses of the term *objective truth* that is endorsed by the court. The first use of objective truth is normally associated with the admissibility of evidence that is perceived as false evidence. For instance, when the witness has provided a declaration that is objectively *not truth*. The second use of the term *objective truth* is associated with an evaluation of the process that retrieves evidence. For instance, the necessity to defend a claim in court might allow illegally obtained evidence that provides a truthful representation of the facts. This is, perhaps, one of the most interesting aspects of the debate over the interplay

---

189 Jerome Frank, *Courts on Trial* (Princeton University Press 1973).

190 For a recent analysis of the whiteness testimony see: Laura Engelhardt, 'The Problem with Eyewitness Testimony' (1999) 1 Stanford Journal of Legal Studies 25.

191 Michel Foucault, *Power/knowledge: Selected Interviews and Other Writings, 1972–1977 /* (Pantheon Books, 1980) 131.

192 Richard Rorty, *Objectivity, Relativism, and Truth* (Cambridge University Press 1991).

193 Rorty (n 29) 1.

between objectivity and truth since it provides a clear distinction between common law systems and civil law systems.[194]

3. Procedural and substantial truths

Having a precise and truthful account of the relevant facts, within the limit of reasonableness,[195] is essential to ensure the quality of judicial decisions in both the civil and common law cases. However, in relation to the regime of illegitimately obtained evidence, continental and English judges adopt different procedural stances. For instance, in Italy, submitting illegitimate evidence in court is generally perceived as antithetical to the deontological functions of the judicial system.[196] In other words, in Italy, the requirement of finding the truth cannot be at the expense of the deontological requirements of the judicial system. The comparison between the English and Italian regimes regarding illegally obtained evidence has been discussed extensively in other sources[197] and it does not need to be reproduced here. In this section, instead I will discuss how the Italian pre-judice associated with illegitimately obtained evidence might have an effect, thus reducing the number of extracts reported in this text that link truth to objectivity.

Italian civil procedures are organized in a code,[198] but the regime of illicitly obtained evidence is largely based on case law.[199] The insistence on excluding, without evaluation, illegitimately obtained evidence, has led researchers to label some civil procedure experts as verofobes.[200] This attitude hinders the functioning of a civil justice system that aspires to providing a truthful interpretation of the facts of the case. From our sample of cases, it is reasonably clear that verophobia is a distinctively Italian phenomenon.

---

194 Breda and Vricella (n 4).

195 See N. MacCormick, Reasonableness and Objectivity, 74 *Notre Dame Law Review* (1998), 1575.

196 M. Taruffo, La Verità nel Processo, *Rivista Trimestrale di Diritto e Procedura Civile* (2012), 1117–1135.

197 Breda and Vricella (n 4).

198 *Codice di Procedura Civile, Royal Decree* n. 1443, 28 September 1940. Please note that the code has been reformed several times.

199 See L. P. Comoglio, Il Problema delle Prove Illecite nell'Esperienza Angloamericana e Germanica (Tipografia del Libro, Pavia 1966).

200 M. Taruffo, Rivista Trimestrale di Diritto e Procedura Civile, (2012), 1117.

In the sample of Italian cases that considered a judicial qualification of the concept of objectivity, the courts did not make a textual reference to the concept of truth. Similar results were also found in the sample of cases from Brazil.[201]

In direct contrast with the Italian casuistry that regulates illicitly obtained evidence, English judges accept most illegally obtained evidence.[202] The reasons for such a difference cannot be pinpointed in this study, but it is important to mention that judges in common law are impartial umpires and they are not expected to interfere in the dispute: 'The passive judicial umpire [in the common law system] is educated on the case by the adversaries, the very parties whose questionable commitment to the truth necessitates judicial participation in the first place.'[203] This increases the pressure on the judiciary to admit all the information that might help with the decision of the case. For instance, one such stance can be seen in family law; English civil procedure includes the so-called *Hildebrand Rules* which de facto encourage one of the spouses, during a divorce, to submit stolen private information that shows the truthful extent of the other spouse's assets.[204] The *Hildebrand Rules* are distinctive to English family law, but a series of precedents greatly reduce the judge's prerogative of evaluating the admissibility of illegally obtained evidence.[205] It is safe to assume that English common law judges are considered impartial arbitrators of disputes in which parties are expected to provide the most persuasive argument and the best correlated evidence to support their claims. This is perceived as the best epistemic method through which to discover the truth (with a small [t]) in a judicial dispute.

---

201 Yves-Andre Faure, 'Jeitinho and Other Related Phenomena in Contemporary Brazil' in Daniel Bach and Mamoudou Gazibo (eds), *Neopatrimonialism in Africa and Beyond* (Routledge 2013).

202 The line of authority is established in: *John Anthony Helliwell and ors. v Terry D. Piggott-Sims*, F.S.R. (1980), 356.

203 Uviller (n 22) 1073.

204 *Hildebrand v Hildebrand*, 1992, 1 FLR 244, Fam. Law, 235. John Anthony Helliwell & ors. v Terry D. Piggott-Sims [1980] FSR 356, Jean F Jones v University of Warwick 2003, EWCA Civ 151.

205 John Anthony Helliwell & ors. v Terry D. Piggott-Sims [1980] FSR 356.

Civil law judges have, by comparison to English judges, a large amount of judicial discretion in disputes over the admissibility of evidence and can ask the party for reports and for the party to undertake other fact-finding activities. However, this investigative power (it is even stronger in criminal law) is balanced by a series of checks and balances aimed at protecting the rights of individuals from abuse by a public institution. These types of limitations are almost inexistent in English law. In England, only an outrageous violation of a right is considered as a potential ground for dismissing the validity of evidence.[206]

4. Interpreting the data: truth as a qualifier of judicial objectivity and verophobia

In the previous section, I discussed the lexical qualification of objective truth in civil and common law systems. The two legal families tend to have a divergent attitude towards the lexical qualification of objective truth in judicial discourse. Even in leading cases such as, John Anthony Helliwell & others v Terry D Piggott-Sims and Jean F Jones v University of Warwick the courts do not use the term *truth* as a qualifier of the term *objectivity*. The lack of enthusiasm for the coupling of the two cannot be explained by considering the two terms as a tautologism. The sample of cases includes instances in which truth is considered as an element of the case. In Porter and another v Magill, for instance, the House of Lords use the term *truth* for rhetorical effect, but the term is not associated with the concept of objectivity.[207] In Joseph and others v Spiller and another, however, the court provides a qualification of the term *Truth*, which is related, albeit indirectly, to the concept of objectivity.[208] Joseph and others v Spiller and another is a libel case. In the English legal system, a slanderous comment might be excused if the comment were truthful or considered as 'a fair statement'.

206 'The weight to be attached to each of the two public interests will vary according to the circumstances. [...] Here, the court cannot ignore the reality of the situation. This is not a case where the conduct of the defendant's insurers is so outrageous that the defence should be struck out.' John Anthony Helliwell & ors. v Terry D. Piggott-Sims p. 962.

207 Porter and another v Magill [2002] 1 All ER 465 490.

208 Joseph and others v Spiller and another [2011] 1 All ER 947.

So the text of the case in Joseph and others v Spiller indirectly qualifies the concept of truth by making reference to previous jurisprudence. In particular, the Supreme Court refers to a 1952 case called Kemsley v Foot.[209] Kemsley v Foot was not included in the sample, but the courts in Kemsley v Foot and Joseph and others v Spiller and another sought to qualify what could be considered truthful for the defendants and not objectively truthful for an English common law court. So the reference to a 'fair comment' could not be considered as objective since it sets, by way of comparison to the judicial perception of an objective statement, a lower threshold. From Table 1 it is possible to derive a correspondence between extract a *(the court refers to facts that are objectively retrieved*) and the judicial activity aimed at qualifying the interplay between truth and objectivity, but this is only related to slanderous comments made by the defendants in libel cases. Similarly, when considering an item in the case to be uncontested because the party agrees that it is so is not a direct qualification of the relationship between truth and objectivity (extract c: *the parties agree on the issue*). The existence of agreements is, instead, a manifestation of judges acting as independent referees in a dispute and not as an institution that establishes ontological truth.

The interplay between judicial objectivity and truth assumes a deontological connotation in civil law systems,[210] but before I continue with the review of the results, it is important to remember that the aim of the study is not to suggest that one judicial system is better than another. The interpretation of the project suggests that legal systems have a different cluster of pre-judices. These pre-judices are criteria that a national community of legal professionals perceive as qualifying the concept of judicial objectivity. In the case of the interplay between objectivity and truth, a quick glance at Table 1 will reveal that some of the national analyses do not consider the two concepts as related. In the case of Italy, there is well-established literature that explains the judicial reticence to couple the concept of truth with the concept of judicial objectivity.[211] This aspect of the project might require an in-depth national study.

209 Kemsley v Foot [1952] 1 All ER 501.
210 Breda and Vricella (n 4).
211 Taruffo (n 13); Breda and Vricella (n 4).

However, the judicial systems that do consider the concept of objectivity as related to the concept of truth have a variety of pre-judices. The samples that report positive responses use the term *truth* to qualify (or to disqualify) external evidence. For instance, in the Slovenian sample, the Supreme Court confirmed the view of the Higher Court on the credibility of a victim's testimony and added that 'other circumstantial evidence and some parts of the defendant's own testimony [...] confirm that [the victim's] testimony was *objectively true* [emphasis added].'[212] It is important to note that in this case the court justified its position by validating the testimony with other evidence that corroborated the victim's account of the events such as photographic material. Another example of the use of the term *objective truth* as a qualifier of factual narratives is in the Lithuanian sample. The Supreme Court of Lithuania confirmed the objective truth of a witness's testimony and opinion, providing an articulated analysis of the reason why the evidence was so closely related to the historical event discussed by the court.[213]

The case sample from Spain provides perhaps the most interesting results for this part of the project. As in the Slovenian and Lithuanian cases, Spanish cases used the terms *objectivity* and *truth* to evaluate evidence.[214] However, in Spain's set of judicial narratives, the *objective truth* is also a manifestation of the court's prerogative to balance the right to a fair process with the right to question witness arguments.[215] In the Spanish decisions, witness statements were considered objectively truthful only if they were supported by factual evidence.[216] In the sample, there is also a distinctive

212 Decision No. KB 2/2009.

213 2011-12-29 No. 2K-617/2011.

214 STS 01/II/11 RJ 2011\1933.

215 For a general analisys of this issues see, for instace, Lorenzo Zucca, *Constitutional Dilemmas: Conflicts of Fundamental Legal Rights in Europe and the USA* (Oxford University Press 2007) 124.

216 STS 21/III/11 RJ 2011\2893); (STS 11/III/11 RJ 2011\2767); (STS 25/II/11 RJ 2011\2481); (STS 16/II/11 RJ 2011\2358); (STS 14/II/11 RJ 2011\2353); (STS 31/I/11 RJ 2011\1807).

difference between the concept of objective judicial truth[217] and that of material truth, which is a scientific evaluation of facts.[218]

The Hungarian sample of cases provides the most articulate range of textual references to a relation between truth and objectivity. The court uses terms such as *objective truth* in twenty-one cases. An interesting analogy between the results taken from the Hungarian sample and the British sample is related to a qualification of objective truth in cases of media communication. In the Judgment of Békés County Court No. P.20199/2009/8, the judge explained that it was unrealistic to expect journalists to ascertain whether the statement of a (third) person corresponded to an objective truth before reporting it.[219] The requirement to check the fairness of information is, instead, one of the requirements of English law.

The Slovakian sample of cases does not include any direct references to a connection between truth and objectivity. It includes, like the UK sample, a small number of instances in which the court makes an indirect qualification of the interplay between the concepts of objectivity and truth.[220] Distinctive of the Slovenian jurisprudence is the evaluation of, for instance, evidence that is associated with an objective truth. In the UK sample of cases, the rhetorical function of a reference to truth is, by way of comparison to the Slovenian cases, more prominent.

I could continue providing examples and the reader can indeed review the project reports on Australia's Academic and Research Network,[221] but I think it is sufficiently clear that even the textual reference to objective truth in judicial discourse is the starting point for a cluster of cognitive activities that distinguish each legal system considered in this project.[222] A unique feature of the coupling between objectivity and truth is the refusal by some legal systems to consider it as a generally accepted judicial concept. That is the deduction that was made having analysed the Italian and the Brazilian sample cases. Even the Slovenian and Slovakian legal systems

217 STS 11/III/11 RJ 2011\2767; STS 01/II/11 RJ 2011\1933.

218 STS 14/II/11 RJ 2011\2353.

219 P.20199/2009/8.

220 CC SR in PL. ÚS 9/07 SC SR; 7So/133/2010; SC 4 Cdo 2/2011).

221 'Australia's Academic and Research Network' <https://www.aarnet.edu.au> accessed 13 August 2016.

222 Legrand (n 12); Legrand (n 5).

yielded a limited number of functional qualifications of the concept of truth and objectivity. This result is relatively inconsistent with the assumption of Coleman and Leiter's idea of a strong metaphysical analysis of factual narratives, which I discussed in the previous chapter.[223] Recall that the evaluations of legal facts are dominated by scientific method and it is reasonable to suggest that such a methodology will deliver objective, reproducible and truthful representations of the circumstances of the case. It is, therefore, reasonable to expect that courts across national legal systems will consider the analysis of factual narratives as scientific truths and a manifestation of strong epistemic practices in natural science. The data from the sample does not confirm such a hypothesis. It appears, instead, that courts across legal systems are reluctant to acknowledge a connection between truth and judicial objectivity. The Italian sample of cases in which the courts qualify the concept of judicial objectivity had no reference to truth. Romania had only three extracts, Lithuania had two. Slovakia and the UK yielded only indirect references in which the word *truth* was not mentioned. The Hungarian sample was the notable exception, with over twenty cases of textual references to objective truth. The study was not designed to evaluate negative results, but the paucity of references to objective truth might suggest that verophobia is also common outside the Italian legal system.[224]

5. Judicial objectivity as a qualifier of fairness and justice

In the previous section, I discussed the use of truth as a qualifier of the concept of objectivity in judicial discourse. In this section of the chapter, I will focus instead on justice. In colloquialisms, truth and justice are often associated as obvious partners but their relationship is only superficial. The point was already made in the second book of Plato's *Republic*: 'Well said, Cephalus, I replied; but as concerning justice, what is it? – To speak the truth and to pay your debts – no more than this? [...] But then, I said, speaking the truth and paying your debts is not a correct definition of justice.'[225] In this part of the *Republic*, Plato introduced a well-known trope to discredit

223 Coleman and Leiter (n 21).
224 Breda and Vricella (n 4); Taruffo (n 13).
225 Plato, *The Republic of Plato* (Allan David Bloom ed, Basic Books 1991) 5.

the traditional and esoteric views of ancient Athens, which were made explicit in the words of the elderly Cephalus. Cephalus's suggestion that truth and justice could be coupled was quickly disenthralled by Socrates, and Cephalus does indeed go back to his sacrifices to the Gods and he is not heard of again. This section of the chapter will not try to revisit Cephalus's mistake. As mentioned earlier, justice and truth are discussed in the same part of the book because our study revealed a handful of cases in which justice was associated with objectivity.

The study revealed that the majority of the contextual uses of the term *objectivity* were related to justice as procedural correctness and fairness.

a. The court applies a rule (which is fair).
b. The court considered an argument to be sufficiently justified.
c. The process is correct (e.g. transparent, balanced).
d. The court evaluates the transfer of rights.

However, the elements of judicial correctness are seldom defined in a way that might satisfy Alexy's own understanding of procedural justice.[226] This group of abstracts is reproduced in the research but it reveals little of what the court perceives as objective because it is fair. More interestingly, by way of comparison, is the court's qualification of the trilateral relation between the terms *fairness*, *justice* and *objectivity*. In particular, this study shows that courts tend to associate with the idea of 'correct procedure'. For instance, in family law, the court seeks a just distribution of resources between the divorcing partners. However, the judicial use of the term *fairness* appears to also have been used with its functional meaning. For instance, fairness is constructed as a synonym of social justice. These types of judicial qualifications that focused on the status of the party in the trial (e.g. the plaintiff is a pensioner or a student) had a relevance in the decision of the case. The sample of cases from Hungary and Slovenia show the process that courts adopt in allocating resources.

However, the sample from the UK has provided the most articulated analysis of the interplay between objectivity, fairness and justice. The analysis of our sample of cases shows that the concept of fairness is deeply

226 Alexy, Adler and MacCormick (n 25); Robert Alexy, 'The Nature of Legal Philosophy' (2004) 17 Ratio Juris 156; Zucca (n 52).

rooted in common law.[227] However, the term *fairness* is associated with an evaluation of the party's claim which might convince the court to impose a monetary transfer. For instance, in Miller v Miller; McFarlane v McFarlane, the House of Lords refers to fairness in its evaluation of the financial implications of short marriages. 'In the case of a short marriage *fairness* might well require that the claimant spouse should not be entitled to a share of the property which the other spouse had brought with him or her into the marriage or acquired by inheritance or gift during the marriage (non-matrimonial property).'[228] The instinctive reaction is to consider the use of fairness as a subjective criterion. The issue is squarely engaged by the House of Lords in Miller v Miller; McFarlane v McFarlane. The court posited that fairness might be a subjective concept:

> *Fairness* is an elusive concept. *It is an instinctive response* to a given set of facts. Ultimately it is grounded in social and moral values. *These values, or attitudes, can be stated. But they cannot be justified, or refuted, by any objective process* of logical reasoning. Moreover, they change from one generation to the next. It is not surprising, therefore, that in the present context there can be different views on the requirements of fairness in any particular case.[229] [Emphasis added]

The level of indeterminacy, the court continues, which is normally associated with fairness is, however, mitigated by external objective factors. These factors, such as the financial needs of the partner who will look after the children, provide an intersubjective set of judicial criteria which might be defined as objective.[230] Fairness is also considered as a socially dependant concept but its pragmatic implications are constructed by the court by reference

---

227 Albert Venn Dicey, 'Development of Administrative Law in England' (1915) 31 LQ Rev. 148, 149; 151. In non-legal analyses fairness is associated with equity but the two terms have a different technical significance in legal narratives. Equity is associated with a prerogative to give common law judges specific remedies (e.g. the restitution of lent items) to the party in a dispute.

228 Miller v Miller; McFarlane v McFarlane [2006] 3 All ER 1 at 7.

229 Ibid.

230 The search is always for the *requirements* of fairness in the particular case. What then, in principle, are these requirements? The statute provides that first consideration shall be given to the welfare of the children of the marriage. In the present context nothing further needs to be said about this primary consideration. *Beyond this several elements, or strands, are readily discernible.* The first is financial needs. This is one of the matters listed in s 25(2)(b): 'the

to objective criteria. In this case, those objective criteria are set in a statute. There is, perhaps, a parallel between the epistemic methodology adopted by the court in McFarlane to qualify *fairness* in a contentious divorce and the *outrageous* violation of privacy rights in John Anthony Helliwell & others v Terry D Piggott-Sims. In both instances, the courts propose a qualification of terms. That is, the adjectives *outrageous* in Helliwell v Piggott and *fair* in McFarlane. However, by making reference to elements that are outside of the case, the two parties argued that terms could be constructed objectively.

6. Interpreting the data: justice, fairness and judicial objectivity

The analysis of the data confirms the existence of multiple judicial qualifications of the interplay between justice, fairness, and objectivity. In Table 1 there is a visual representation of the matrix formed by a contextual analysis of the extracts.

The court asserts that its decision is objectively *fair* or *just* because:

a. the court applies a rule;
b. the court considered an argument to be sufficiently justified;
c. the process is correct (e.g. transparent, balanced);
d. the court evaluates the transfer of rights.

The extracts are taken from a small number of cases, and some judicial systems do not appear to qualify the relationship between the three concepts. For instance, the Brazilian and Spanish samples of cases did not make even a single direct textual reference to the relation between judicial objectivity and fairness. The Italian and Lithuanian samples yielded only one case each.

So there is, by way of comparison to the analysis of judicial bias, a limited amount of data. However, it is clear that the British and the Slovakian common law have the most articulated qualification of the relation between fairness and judicial objectivity. These large variations are not indicative of the quality of judicial narratives. They are, however, indicative of the

financial needs, obligations and responsibilities which each of the parties to the marriage has or is likely to have in the foreseeable future'. Ibid at 8.

existence of national distinctive pre-judices and of the large variations in the judicial narrative across judicial systems.

Furthermore, these judicial narratives correspond to a group of qualifications. The first group of qualifications provides a justification for compensating a party in a dispute. The second group of judicial narratives is instead a manifestation of social justice. In this group of cases, the court evaluates how public resources are allocated to individuals. The third is populated by the judicial evaluation of procedural aspects of the case.

The first group of qualifications includes cases such as the one from the Balassagyarmat County Court in Hungary: '[I]t violates the principle of objective justice, if the defendant has to compensate those people, who did not act in a way that could generally be expected from them (to avoid suffering damages).'[231] The court, in this case, considers unfair the request for compensation by a plaintiff who did not behave in the way that would have been expected from a reasonable individual. Included in this group of qualifications is the UK House of Lords decision Re Byfield (a bankrupt), ex parte Hill Samuel & Co Ltd v The trustee of the bankrupt in which the court applies the principle of fairness as a criterion for allocating resources after bankruptcy: 'Applying the principle of fairness and honesty and honourable dealing, it seems to me that I ought only to give the trustee the amount which has been paid in as the debtor's property, subject to deduction of the amount to which the estate has benefited.'[232] Another qualification of the term *fairness* in English common law is on the aforementioned Miller v Miller; McFarlane v McFarlane. The two cases were bounded in a single decision and the House of Lords was given the task of providing an objective qualification of the fair redistribution of wealth between two divorcees.[233] As I mentioned in previous parts of this book, the narratives in Miller v Miller; McFarlane v McFarlane are the manifestation of a distinctively British epistemic methodology that fits well with, for instance, Coleman's idea of modest objectivity.[234] In these types of judicial qualifications, the court's opinions tend to provide a pragmatic qualification of a general term, such

231 no. P.20362/2007/17.

232 [1982] 1 All ER 249, p. 253.

233 Miller v Miller; McFarlane v McFarlane [2006] UKHL 24.

234 Coleman and Leiter (n 21).

as fairness, without engaging the theoretical analysis. The result is often an intersubjective rendering of concepts which might be perceived as objective only from an internal national perspective.[235]

The second group of judicial narratives that connects justice with objectivity focuses on the allocation of public resources or the distinctive status of those affected by the judicial decision. For example, as the Supreme Court of Slovenia explained, this principle requires 'taking into account *society's objective material capabilities* [emphasis added] [...] and the jurisprudence/case law of the courts in similar cases.'[236] The court's opinion is particularly interesting because in evaluating a legal dispute, the court balances a functional aspect of government (that is, how public resources are allocated) and the requirement of justice.

The third group of qualifications of the terms *justice*, *fairness* and *objective* is squarely procedural. These types of qualifications tend to focus on the strict adherence to the step-by-step process of delivering justice inside and outside the court. In this group of cases, the most interesting example is taken from the Slovakian sample. The Constitutional Court discussed the election of the General Prosecutor. One of the candidates claimed that the election was not just because the Members of Parliament were taking pictures of their votes while voting in the secret ballot. It is logical to assume that such a practice was a manifestation of the party's orders.

The Constitutional Court held that election process was not conducted objectively because it did not give an equal chance of participation to all the voters. A similar evaluation of procedural fairness is discussed by the House of Lords in R (on the application of Animal Defenders International) v Secretary of State for Culture, Media and Sport. In this case, the court evaluated the procedural fairness of government policy. The court explained that:

> Chapter 4 of Pt 3 contains regulatory provisions and sections 319–328 are directed to programme and fairness standards for television and radio. Section 319 *requires* that Office of Communications (OFCOM), a supervisory body established by s 1 of the *Act, set standards to achieve a number of objectives, among them that news is reported with due impartiality and accuracy* and, in sub-s (2)(g), that advertising

235 Legrand (n 5) 51.
236 My Epmphasys', Decision No. II Ips 353/2007.

> which contravenes the prohibition on political advertising set out in s 321(2) is not included in television or radio services. Section 320 requires that programmes should, within a given programme or over a number of *programmes taken as a whole or a series, preserve due impartiality in relation to matters of political or industrial controversy and matters relating to current public policy.*[237]

The House of Lords, in this case, evaluated the fairness of the procedure adopted by OFCOM evaluating broadcasted public information. The issue, in this case, was whether OFCOM had complied with the procedures that guarantee unbiased information. Again, the violation of the procedure was tantamount to an injustice.

7. Conclusion: truth, objectivity and justice

Truth, justice and objectivity are words that are often used as synonyms and as reciprocal preconditions. They often bring a warm glow to a discussion. In this chapter, I discussed their lexical and epistemic interplay by focusing on judicial narratives. Judicial truth is, our analysis suggests, a small [t] truth that leans heavily on procedural fairness. The analysis also explained that truth has a different type of importance in common and civil law systems. Italian leading researchers, such as Taruffo, used the term *verofobes* to describe the general attitude of the Italian judges. His narratives also show a twinge of dismay at the unfettered fatuity of Italian judicial narratives.

The common law system is, on a general level, more concerned with an objective representation of the facts of the case, yet this is at the expense of the protection of rights. The second part of the chapter engaged the triangular interplay between objectivity, fairness and justice. There is no plausible connection between truth and justice. This part of the study revealed a tendency to construct fairness and justice as a procedural concept. However, the assertion of pernicious procedural aspects of the case is seldom qualified. In other words, procedural problems are perceived *ipso facto* as hindering justice. The most interesting results of this part of the project are the qualifications of justice as fairness in the English, Slovakian and Romanian cases. In all these legal systems, justice is associated with a well-articulated concept of fairness.

---

237 Emphasis added [2008] 3 All ER 193 p. 198.

Bibliography

Alexy R, 'The Nature of Legal Philosophy' (2004) 17 Ratio juris 156

Alexy R, Adler R and MacCormick N, *A Theory of Legal Argumentation: The Theory of Rational Discourse as Theory of Legal Justification* (Oxford University Press 2009)

Azuelos-Atias S, 'Semantically Cued Contextual Implicatures in Legal Texts' (2010) 42 Journal of Pragmatics 728

Breda V and Vricella M, 'English Pragmatism and Italian Virtue: A Comparative Analysis of the Regime of Illegally Obtained Evidence in Civil Law Proceedings between Italy and England' (2014) 21 Maastricht Journal of European and Comparative Law 428

Capell HL, 'After the Glass Has Shattered: A Comparative Analysis of Orthodox Jewish Divorce in the United States and Israel' (1998) 33 Tex. Int'l LJ Texas International Law Journal 331

Coleman JL and Leiter B, 'Determinacy, Objectivity, and Authority' (1993) University of Pennsylvania Law Review 549

Dicey AV, 'Development of Administrative Law in England' (1915) 31 LQ Rev. 148

Engelhardt L, 'The Problem with Eyewitness Testimony' (1999) 1 Stanford Journal of Legal Studies 25

Faure Y-A, 'Jeitinho and Other Related Phenomena in Contemporary Brazil' in Daniel Bach and Mamoudou Gazibo (eds), *Neopatrimonialism in Africa and Beyond* (Routledge 2013)

Finnis J, *Natural Law and Natural Rights* (Oxford University Press 2011)

Foucault M, *Power/knowledge: Selected Interviews and Other Writings, 1972–1977 /* (Pantheon Books, 1980)

Frank J, *Courts on Trial* (Princeton University Press 1973)

Goldman AI, *Knowledge in a Social World* (Clarendon Press 1999)

Keane A, *The Modern Law of Evidence* (Oxford University Press 2008)

Langacker R, *Foundations of Cognitive Grammar: Volume II: Descriptive Application* (Stanford University Press 1991)

Legrand P, 'European Legal Systems Are Not Converging' (1996) 45 The International and Comparative Law Quarterly 52

_, 'Against a European Civil Code' (1997) 60 The Modern Law Review 44

Levine A, *Economic Morality and Jewish Law* (Oxford University Press 2012)

Plato, *The Republic of Plato* (Allan David Bloom ed, Basic Books 1991)

Rawls J, 'The Idea of Public Reason' in William Rehg (ed), *Deliberative democracy: essays on reason and politics* (MIT 1997)

_, 'Justice as Fairness: Political Not Metaphysical", Philosophy and Public Affairs, 14 (3), Summer, 223-51' (1998) 97 International Library of Critical Writings in Economics 250

_, *Political Liberalism* / (Expanded ed, Columbia University Press, 2005)

Rorty R, *Objectivity, Relativism, and Truth* (Cambridge University Press 1991)

Tadros V, 'Enabling Proceduralism' in Emilios A Christodoulidis and Stephen Tierney (eds), *Public Law and Politics: the scope and limits of constitutionalism* (Ashgate 2008)

Taruffo M, 'La Verità Nel Processo' [2012] Rivista Trimestrale di Diritto e Procedura Civile 1117

Uviller R, 'Advocate, the Truth, and Judicial Hackles: A Reaction to Judge Frankel's Idea' (1975) 123 University of Pennsylvania Law Review 1067

Wincott D, 'Reshaping Public Space? Devolution and Policy Change in British Early Childhood Education and Care' (2005) 15 Regional and Federal Studies 453

Zucca L, *Constitutional Dilemmas: Conflicts of Fundamental Legal Rights in Europe and the USA* (Oxford University Press 2007)

Chapter 3
Objective judicial discretion cases

1. Introduction

As mentioned throughout this book, judicial narratives have to be perceived as objective and the existence of a pre-existing clear and specific rule provides the argument *par excellence* to support an objective judicial decision.[238] However, in cases in which the court is asked to evaluate new legal dilemmas or cases that are seen as being within the so-called Hartian penumbra, the perception of judicial objectivity tends to be more difficult to defend. This chapter discussed the range of epistemic methods that judges adopt in cases in which there is no predetermined explicit legal rule. I called these types of instances *judicial discretion cases*. As in the rest of this book, the analysis relied on the cognitive textual analysis of a large sample of national cases. The textual narratives of these cases were analysed using Langacker's methodology that is adapted to a legal analysis.[239] The nine legal systems that were considered include Brazil, Hungary, Italy, Lithuania, Romania, Spain, Slovakia, Slovenia and the UK.

On the linear scale that connects hard cases with difficult cases, judicial discretion cases tend to be closer to the former than to the latter. For instance, in a judicial discretion case, the court might be asked to decide which administrative process, from among a number of equivalent processes that deliver the same objective, might better implement a government policy. The analysis of the extract and its cognitive use shows that judges seek to deliver, in each

---

238 Neil MacCormick, *Legal Reasoning and Legal Theory* (Clarendon Press 1994) ix, 19–29.

239 Ronald Langacker, *Foundations of Cognitive Grammar: Volume II: Descriptive Application* (Stanford University Press 1991); Izabela Skoczeń, 'Minimal Semantics and Legal Interpretation' [2015] International Journal for the Semiotics of Law - 1, 3; Marek Zirk-Sadowski, 'Interpretation of Law and Judges Communities' (2012) 25 International Journal for the Semiotics of Law - 473; Vito Breda, 'The Grammar of Bias: Judicial Impartiality in European Legal Systems' [2016] International Journal for the Semiotics of Law -, First Online 2016-7-25.

case, the most plausible evaluation of factual and legal narratives that are perceived as acceptable by the national community of legal professionals. These accepted epistemological assumptions support, as discussed earlier, Coleman and Leiter's idea of modest objectivity in law.[240] The study also shows how there are several national variations between judicial methodologies, which again confirms the existence of national pre-judices. In cases of judicial discretion, pre-judices are manifested in chosen epistemic practices which a national legal community of legal professionals perceived as being within the limits of a legitimated decision. Distinctive of the objective discretion cases is their role in closing a lacuna in the legal system. It is important to remember that the doctrine of stare decisis differentiates civil and common law systems only to a degree.[241] Civil judges are also obliged to provide consistent decisions (the so-called horizontal effect of the doctrine of the binding precedent) and to comply with the jurisprudence of the final appellate jurisdictions (the so-called vertical effect of a precedent).[242]

Also distinctive to objective discretion cases is the range of cognitive methods adopted by different judges.[243] The lack of consistency between legal systems – some of which are part of the same legal family and have a very similar historical development (such as Spain and Italy) – does not disprove the role of objectivity in cases of judicial discretion. The analysis of the judicial argument from objectivity shows, instead, the existence of a dynamic conception of objectivity which resembles what Coleman and Leiter call *modest objectivity*.[244] In particular, an analysis of the sample

240 Jules L Coleman and Brian Leiter, 'Determinacy, Objectivity, and Authority' [1993] University of Pennsylvania Law Review 549.

241 *See* Jan Komárek, 'Reasoning with Previous Decisions: Beyond the Doctrine of Precedent' (2013) 61 American Journal of Comparative Law 149, 149, 160–167, 170.

242 *See* Vincy Fon and Francesco Parisi, 'Judicial Precedents in Civil Law Systems: A Dynamic Analysis' (2006) 26 International Review of Law and Economics. 519; Marco Croce, 'Precedente Giudiziale E Giurisprudenza Costituzionale' (2006) 4 1114; Rodolfo Sacco, 'Legal Formants: A Dynamic Approach to Comparative Law' (1991) 39 The American Journal of Comparative Law 343, 356.

243 Pierre Legrand, 'Against a European Civil Code' (1997) 60 The Modern Law Review 44, 51.

244 Coleman and Leiter (n 3).

of cases tends to indicate an institutional concern with equanimity and independence.[245]

The chapter is divided into two sections that are preceded by an introduction and followed by a conclusion. Section 2 discusses the theoretical debate surrounding objective judicial discretion cases and Section 3 provides an overview of the results.

2. A theoretical overview

This chapter discusses cases in which the courts have discretion and refer to the concept of judicial objectivity to support their decisions. For instance, the sample includes cases in which Spanish administrative courts were asked to decide which expert witness report, among a series of documents drafted by different experts and supporting different conclusions, was to be considered as binding.[246] The court, in selecting the witness report that it considers binding, is not acting in a complete vacuum. It must, like I discussed in the case of responding to an allegation of bias, adopt an epistemic methodology that is perceived as adequate by the majority of the legal professionals in that legal system.[247] These pre-judices might also be distinctive of areas of law within a legal system, but that hypothesis was not tested in this study.

Empirical analyses on the law of the judicial process seldom bring good news to theorists. Empirical evaluations of judicial decisions have indicated unexplainable discrepancies concerning the judicial process. The list of external factors that might change a judicial process range from the trivial, such as the lack of a good breakfast for the judge, to the disturbing, such as institutional racism. For instance, Shai Danziger, Jonathan Levav and Liora Avnaim-Pesso suggest that the level of tiredness of a judge might

245 MacCormick (n 1); Neil MacCormick, 'Reasonableness and Objectivity' (1998) 74 Notre Dame Law Review 1575; Maksymilian Del Mar, 'The Forward-Looking Requirement of Formal Justice: Neil MacCormick on Consequential Reasoning' (2015) 6 Jurisprudence 429.

246 Komárek (n 4); Fon and Parisi (n 5).

247 Coleman and Leiter (n 3); Pierre Legrand, 'European Legal Systems Are Not Converging' (1996) 45 The International and Comparative Law Quarterly 52; Legrand (n 6).

decrease the rate of conviction by as much as 65%.[248] What would appear to be less humorous are those external factors that show an indication of racial, political, and gender bias.[249] The results of their analysis fuelled the realist movement and many of the so-called nihilist perspectives in law, such as the one promoted by critical legal studies (CLS) and by the Critical Race Theory.[250]

In the introduction and in chapter 1, I mentioned the CLS's contribution to the theoretical debate over the allegation of judicial bias. One of the issues that has frustrated critical legal theorists is the cleavage between the claim made by, for instance, the *law in the book* and the *law in action*. In particular, critical movements rejected the claim of the objectivity of the decisional process, arguing that it was affected, at best, by random factors, as proved by studies such as the one by Shai Danziger and others,[251] or at worst, by sinister ideological assumptions, as suggested by Oren Gazal-Ayal and Raanan Sulitzeanu-Kenan.[252] The general implications of this group of analyses are well summarised by Coleman and Leiter: 'According to CLS, the

---

248 S. Danziger, J. Levav, L. Avnaim-Pesso, *Extraneous Factors in Judicial Decisions*, (2011) 108 Proceedings of the National Academy of Sciences of the United States of America, 6889; A. Kozinski, 'What I Ate for Breakfast and other Mysteries of Judicial Decision Making', (*1992*) *26 Loy. LAL Review*, 993.

249 O. Gazal-Ayal, R. Sulitzeanu-Kenan, 'Let My People Go: Ethnic In-Group Bias in Judicial Decisions—Evidence from a Randomized Natural Experiment', *(2010) 7 Journal of Empirical Legal Studies,* 403; G. Douglas, J. Pearce, H. Woodward, 'Cohabitants, Property and the Law: A Study of Injustice', (2009) *72 Modern Law Review,* 24.

250 Coleman and Leiter (n 3) 549. For a general overview of the CLS's stance on judicial objectivity, see: Michael Hardt and Antonio Negri, *Empire* (Harvard University Press 2000); Costas Douzinas and Adam Gearey, *Critical Jurisprudence: The Political Philosophy of Justice* (Hart 2005); Emilios Christodoulidis, *Law and Reflexive Politics* (Kluwer 1998). For an introduction to critical race theory: Robert Post and Michael Paul Rogin, *Race and Representation: Affirmative Action* (Zone Books 1998); Post and Rogin; Derrick A Bell, 'Who's Afraid of Critical Race Theory' (1995) University of Illinois Law Review 893; Richard Delgado, *Critical Race Theory: An Introduction* (2nd ed, New York University Press 2012).

251 S. Danziger, Levav and Avnaim-Pesso (n 11).

252 O. Gazal-Ayal and Sulitzeanu-Kenan (n 12).

problem with liberalism is that none of these ideals obtain in legal practice. Law is neither determinate nor objective nor neutral.'[253] Perhaps one of the most detailed analyses of the ideological colonisation of the judiciary is in Rigaux's historical evaluation of the impact of Nazism in German criminal law.[254] Rigaux explained that while the German criminal procedures were comparable to the ones adopted in other European systems, after the establishment of Nazism, German judges commenced to insert ideological elements into their jurisprudence.[255] This was particularly evident in cases in which the court used analogy to cover a statutory lacuna.[256] That was the case, for instance, in the criminal convictions of individuals who were involved in crimes against political opponents of the emerging regime.[257] This study has not found evidence of ideological incursions that are analogous to the ones described by Rigaux.[258] This might have to do with the type of decision. Objective discretion cases are analogous to what Hart calls *penumbra cases*.[259] In these cases, there are no clear rules, but their decision process is reasonably restricted. Hart describes this process in a succinct narrative:

> Instead of saying that the recurrence of penumbral questions shows us that legal rules are essentially incomplete, and that, when they fail to determine decisions, judges must legislate and so exercise a creative choice between alternatives, we shall say that the social policies which guide the judges' choice are in a sense there for them to discover; the judges are only 'drawing out' of the rule what, if it is properly understood, is 'latent' within it. To call this judicial legislation is to obscure some essential continuity between the clear cases of the rule's application and the penumbral decisions.[260]

A court that is called to decide a case in which it has discretion might, for instance, reference to government schemes. However, the reference by a judge

---

253 J. Coleman and Leiter (n 3) 549.
254 François Rigaux, *La Loi Des Juges* (Jacob 1997) 96–98, 105.
255 Rigaux (n 17) 107–109.
256 Rigaux (n 17) 107.
257 Rigaux (n 17).
258 Rigaux (n 17) 97.
259 HLA Hart, 'Positivism and the Separation of Law and Morals' (1958) 71 Harvard Law Review 593; Lon L Fuller, 'Positivism and Fidelity to Law: A Reply to Professor Hart' (1958) 71 Harvard Law Review 630.
260 H.L.A. Hart, 'Positivism and the Separation of Law and Morals', *(1958) 71 Harvard Law Review* 593, 612.

to the government's commitment to implementing a policy is a manifestation of one of the epistemic methods that the court perceived as relevant in the decision of a case.[261] In other words, it is not an indication that courts are politically biased. This point is made by Coleman and Leiter in a succinct narrative:

> No analytic jurisprudence – not Dworkin, not Hart, not Fuller, not Raz, nor anyone else – has ever referred to his or her jurisprudence as 'liberal'. This is so in spite of the fact that Dworkin, Hart, and Raz are arguably amongst the most important figures in political liberalism of the last half of this century.[262]

It could be argued that a lack of any direct references to liberalism is no guarantee of a 'liberalism-free' theory of law. It could be suggested, for instance, that Hart tried to project his set of beliefs, unconsciously or surreptitiously, onto others. This argument is, however, far-fetched.

Coleman and Leiter suggest, instead, that both legal realism and CLS misconstrued the partnership between liberalism and adjudication by considering liberal jurisprudential accounts of law, like Hart's projection, which were tinted with determinism. This is a controversial point, so I must be precise. The two authors do not argue that liberalism is not a political ideology; rather, they suggest that, as a compressive doctrine, it is committed to objectivity. In particular, they argue that liberalism promotes an idea of modest objectivity in law. Modest objectivity in judicial practices seeks to project the pragmatic limitations of the judicial process under an ideal epistemic condition. The advantage of Coleman and Leiter's concept of *modest objectivity* is firstly the decoupling of the judicial practice from its results. In other words, legal narratives are not part of an ideological fiefdom. Secondly, and perhaps as a corollary of the first point, judicial objectivity as a pragmatic concept should be separated from universalist aspirations.[263]

---

261 James Boyle, 'The Politics of Reason: Critical Legal Theory and Local Social Thought' (1985) 133 University of Pennsylvania Law Review 685, n. 29.

262 J. Coleman, B. Leiter, 'Determinacy, Objectivity, and Authority', op. cit. (n 3), 553.

263 Coleman and Leiter (n 3) 621; Nicholas Evans and Stephen C Levinson, 'The Myth of Language Universals: Language Diversity and Its Importance for Cognitive Science' (2009) 32 Behavioral and Brain Sciences 429.

Modest objectivity might explain, for instance, the systematic inconstancies reported by empirical studies such as the one by Danziger but, more importantly for our debate, it provides a paradigm that might explain the variety of epistemic methods adopted in objective judicial discretion cases. In particular, textual analysis based on the principle of cognitive grammar shows that arguments from objectivity are a proxy for a larger spectrum of epistemic methodologies.[264] The segment of epistemic method might include a reference to objective technical analysis, objective collective goals, or a reasonable person. The term *segment* is 'borrowed from statistical analyses and it is intended to explain interdependent overlapping preferences linked to a series of variables. For instance, individuals might have a range of independent preferences (e.g. which car they like most) that are linked to a set of variables (e.g. which job they do and where they do it); the combination of the two allows for a statistical range of options that link the two groups of variables.[265]

In our sample, the court was asked to evaluate a difficult case for which there was no apparent rule. The study indicates, firstly, that courts seek to select from a range of epistemic practices, and secondly that the choice is motivated by an attempt to reach, within the realm of reasonableness, an objective decision. The epistemic methodologies adopted form a cluster of lexical explanations that are distinctive of a national legal system. Again, the variation in clusters of explanations appears to support the idea of Legrand's pre-judices, which I defined in the previous section.[266]

The cluster is made by a combination of textual references which acknowledges the lacunae in the legal system (e.g. the court references to academic/professional studies that reduce the subjective character of a decision) and then combines it with a series of epistemic activities (e.g. the evaluation of expert reports). So, the cluster of lexical narratives combined with a distinctive series of epistemic activities (within the range of activities that are perceived as appropriate by the community of legal professionals) forms a

---

264 For a general review of the cognitive grammar analysis see, for instance: Langacker (n 2).

265 S. Goyat, 'The Basis of Market Segmentation: A Critical Review of Literature', *(2011) 3 European Journal of Business and Management*, 45.

266 Legrand (n 10) 61.

distinctive national matrix. The matrix is a manifestation of national prejudices which constrain judicial decisions in a way that is compatible with Coleman and Leiter's idea of modest objectivity in law.

Before I move on to the analysis, a series of clarifications is necessary. Firstly, the study adopted a hermeneutic approach which focused on the qualification of the meaning of objectivity in the judicial discourse. A more detailed analysis can be found in the methodological section, but, in this chapter, it is important to recall that each researcher worked independently and focused only on her/his legal system. The project also asked researchers to evaluate the meaning of objectivity by focusing on the functional use of the term in legal discourse and its family of resemblance. The analysis relied, as mentioned earlier, on the criteria suggested in Langacker's cognitive grammar, which seeks to determine the conceptual meaning of a word by inserting it in a cluster of narratives.[267] Those narratives define the level of judicial autonomy of a national system. For instance, the term *objective* has different meanings in cases in which judges are asked to evaluate intersubjective concepts such as the reasonable person or external criteria such as a policy aim. To avoid the development of an artificially constructed meaning that was shared by the researchers, the results were only shared at the end of the project and the research was peer reviewed externally.[268]

Secondly, objective judicial discretion cases are not cases in which there is a conflict over fundamental constitutional rights.[269] These types of conflicts might require balancing[270] and a speculative analysis regarding the key role of the legal system.[271] In the large majority of objective judicial discretion cases, judicial discretion is linked to missing rules that can be retrieved by,

---

267 R. Langacker (n 2).

268 Breda (n 2); Vito Breda and Lidia Rodak (eds), *Diverse Narratives of Legal Objectivity: An Interdisciplinary Perspective* (Peter Lang 2016).

269 Lorenzo Zucca, *Constitutional Dilemmas: Conflicts of Fundamental Legal Rights in Europe and the USA* (Oxford University Press 2007).

270 R. Alexy, 'Constitutional Rights, Balancing, and Rationality', *(2003) 16 Ratio Juris,* 131.

271 J. Coleman and Leiter (n 3); Ronald Dworkin, *Taking Rights Seriously* (Harvard University Press 1978); Ronald Dworkin, *Law's Empire* (Fontana 1986).

for instance, using an analogic reasoning or by formulating an evaluation of factual narratives.[272]

3. The analysis of the results

In the previous section, I discussed the theoretical assumptions that inform the debate over objective judicial discretion cases. In these cases, 'there is no specific rule to follow', so to speak, and judges have a higher – by comparison to an ideally constructed clear case – margin of discretion. The textual analysis of objective judicial discretion cases shows that objectivity is normally linked to an epistemic activity which might include an evaluation of technical issues, collective goals, or intersubjective criteria (e.g. the reasonable person). The combination of these processes made up a national group of preferred pre-judices.[273]

The subgroups of extracts were, in turn, divided into three groups:

a. The court references to academic/professional studies to reduce the subjective character of a decision;
b. The court decides that its activity is objective; or
c. The court mixes narratives from points a and b.

As for the rest of this study, negative variations, in which the court defined what could not be associated with the concept of objectivity, were considered as false positives. The second stage of the study included a contextual analysis of the *extracts*. This activity had the aim of *labelling* their cognitive use by the court. This methodology is, as mentioned in the introduction, a common epistemic practice in the cognitive analysis of judicial decisions.[274]

The results of the analyses of the objective discretion cases confirms the analyses of other macro-groups of significance and other similar semantic

272 G. Lamond, 'Analogical Reasoning in the Common Law', *(2014) Oxford Journal of Legal Studies*, Published online first: June 24, 2014.

273 Legrand (n 6) 51.

274 Skoczeń (n 2); Sol Azuelos-Atias, 'Semantically Cued Contextual Implicatures in Legal Texts' (2010) 42 Journal of Pragmatics 728; Langacker (n 2); Breda (n 2).

studies.[275] In particular, an analysis of the national samples of cases suggests the existence of three distinctive groups of pre-judices. I call the first group of cognitive uses *explicit segmented epistemology group*. These are cases in which the court has discretion and it uses the term *objectivity* to qualify its analysis. However, the cognitive process is explained in a series of articulated passages. In other words, the qualification of a decision as objective is coupled with a step-by-step explanation of the cognitive process adopted by the court. The *external segmented epistemology groups* includes cases in which the court explains its decision by making reference to external evidence (e.g. technical reports). The third segment, which I called the *internal segmented epistemology group*, includes objective judicial discretion cases that were decided by making reference to intersubjective objective assumptions (e.g. the concept of reasonableness).

a) Pre-judices: explicit segmented epistemology

The explicit segmented epistemology groups include decisions that might be considered atypical. One of the assumptions of modern legal theory is that judges should choose the argument that provides a strong link between submitted evidence and a legal narrative.[276] It is a well-known pedagogical trope, passed on to several generations of common law students, to depict the judicial process as the decision made by an individual in a dark room where only the beam of light brought by evidence overlaps with the beam of light of the legal argument. The overlap between factual and legal narratives is, in the great majority of cases, considered as determining the outcome of the case. However, in cases in which the overlap between the evidence and narrative might not be as clear, judges do have discretion. This is a case of narrow judicial discretion and relative indeterminacy.[277] Within the group of cases in which the court has some level of discretion, the study show

---

275 Evans and Levinson (n 26); Stephen C Levinson, *Pragmatics* (Cambridge University Press 1983).

276 Ronald Dworkin, *A Matter of Principle* (Harvard University Press 1985) 119; HLA Hart, *The Concept of Law* (Clarendon Press 1961) chs 4–5; HLA Hart, *The Concept of Law* (Penelope Bulloch and Joseph Raz eds, 2nd edition, Oxford University Press 1997) postscript.

277 Coleman and Leiter (n 3) 561.

judges might plainly explain the epistemic method that they have chosen for their decisions. I called these cases explicit cognitive epistemic cases. An explicit cognitive epistemic decision includes an explanation of the criteria adopted to answer the claim under review and sometimes the general consequences that such a decision might have in future cases.

For instance, the Slovakian sample of cases provides several examples of explicit epistemic practices.[278] In cases No. II. ÚS 9/00 and No. III. ÚS 23/00, the Slovakian Constitutional Court had to decide how to interpret two expert reports that purported diverging conclusions. The Constitutional Court explained that, in these circumstances, it had to provide a common interpretation of diverging technical analyses and it listed the cognitive methods that were adopted to support the final decision. An analogous example of manifest epistemic practice is in Decision n. 432 of the Italian Constitutional Court. The court set out the criteria that have to be used by public institutions in case they wish to allocate a service to foreign disabled residents. Decision n. 432 explained the cognitive processes that were to be used in distinguishing the constitutional rights for citizens and the constitutional rights for all. In particular, it explained that foreign residents could not be unreasonably discriminated against by regional institutions. Decision n. 432 is a landmark case that is likely to influence future epistemic practices within Italian jurisprudence.[279] Decision n. 432 is one of a few instances in which the courts adopted an open epistemic methodology. Open epistemic cases are also rare in the group of judicial discretion cases extracted from the UK sample of cases. In the English sample, which is taken from the Supreme Court, the process of evaluation is labelled as objective, yet there is little in the way of information regarding how those objective evaluations are carried out. The clarification of an objective evaluation might require further investigation such as a series of semi-structured interviews with the judges.

In addition, it was not an aim of the study to compare former communist legal systems and old democracies. The Italian sample yielded only

278 no. III. ÚS 47/05, no. III. ÚS 74/2011, III. ÚS 110/07, no. III. ÚS 158/08, no. III. ÚS 198/09. Similarly, no. IV. ÚS 38/09, no. IV. ÚS 303/2010, no. IV. ÚS 292/2010 no. 10Sža/24/2011 no. IV. ÚS 107/2010.

279 n. *432 2005* [2005] G U 07122005 N 49 5.2.

one instance. The Lithuanian, Slovakian and Slovenia samples of cases, however, tend to include a higher number of open segmented epistemic cases. The reason for this divergence is again a matter of speculation, but it is possible to assume that some systems consider the transparency of the judicial process more important than others do. It might be that communism has brought about that requirement of transparency, yet it is outside the remit of this project to analyse it. Or maybe post-communist judges, some of whom recycled themselves in the new regime after being hideous instruments of the old one, are under pressure to appear objective (that is, *not communist*) and wanted to show it in their writings. That would then be a case of the zealousness of the converted. As mentioned earlier, these debates are outside the research's remit.

b) External segmented epistemology

In judicial discretion cases, the courts make reference to external cognitive criteria. Once the external criteria are referred to by a legal narrative, it becomes *by proxy* a part of an accepted narrative that holds a persuasive value in a distinctive legal system. For instance, some of the sociological references, such as the reasonable man in the English legal system, have become deeply embedded in the judicial discourse.[280] Indeed the criteria might appear to be external, but it is part of a shared perception that a community of legal professionals consider 'external',[281] and the sample of cases confirms that *external to law aspects* in a judicial qualification of objectivity is normally a technical or sociological qualification. For instance, decision No. I Ips 186/2009 of the Supreme Court of Slovenia overturned a previous criminal conviction associated with religious sectarianism. In decision No. I Ips 186/2009, the court referred to a sociological analysis to suggest that theistic narratives cannot be considered offensive by those who are agnostic because an independent observer (that represents an external sociological criterion) should not be offended by the sharing of theistic views. In the Spanish sample, two administrative cases are instead decided on the basis of a technical objective urbanistic

280 Note that our sample relied on UK Supreme Court Cases which did not include Scottish private law.
281 Coleman and Leiter (n 3) 567.

criterion.[282] In both cases STS 13/IV/11; 21/II/11 and STS 21/I/11, the parties submitted expert reports that had diverging conclusions. The court had to find an objective accommodation which complied with the collective aim of urban planning under review. A reference to a collective aim is also found in the sample of Brazilian cases.[283] The court had to choose an external epistemic process that could define a collective activity or a collective inactivity. Again, the concept of collective activity was referred to as an external element of the epistemic process that helps the decision of the case. It is reasonable to suggest that in these instances, judges do indeed choose an external epistemic methodology that helps them to qualify a legal reasoning as objective, yet the external criteria manifest a cognitive method that is perceived, at the very least, as acceptable by the community of legal professionals.

c) Internal segmented epistemology

In the previous section, I discussed judicial discretion cases in which the court has limited discretion in evaluating the facts of the case. There is evidence, from the sample considered, that judges have a tendency to accommodate diverging factual narratives (some of which are technical) by making reference to an objective epistemic methodology. Internal legal epistemological references, such as a reasonable man, are not made in a way that is analogous to some Hezekiah–Sennacherib narratives in which a judge seeks to reach an implausible convergence of opinions over the exegetic nature of, for instance, the reasonable person. The textual analysis of the sample indicates, instead, that the chosen epistemology might change in relation to the legal issue.[284]

The variety of lexical expressions and criteria adopted by the courts indicates the existence of a group of epistemic methodologies that is used as reference in an ideal epistemic situation. For instance, in the English legal system, a textual analysis of the cases considered in this project shows that references to the *reasonable person* are uncoupled from a sociological narrative. For instance, the well-known cliché of the male English passenger who is wearing

282 STS 13/IV/11; 21/II/11; STS 21/I/11.
283 ADI-MC 2332; ADI-MC 1717; ADI-MC 1516; MI 562; MI 20; RHC 50828.
284 Richard Rorty, *Objectivity, Relativism, and Truth* (Cambridge University Press 1991) 1.

a black bowler on the Chapman Omnibus is not perceived as a manifestation of the reasonable person in English law.[285] The British reasonable person and the good *pater familias* are mildly complex cognitive constructions that are perceived as an internal element of the judicial reasoning.[286]

The internal nature of these criteria is also asserted in decisions such as No. 3K-3-184/2011 by the Supreme Court of Lithuania: 'The court evaluates all the evidences [...] based on a thorough and objective process of examination of all the circumstances that were presented by the parties during the hearing of the case.'[287] The term *reasonable behaviour* as a qualifier of the concept of objectivity (*ésszerű magatartás*) also appears in the Hungarian sample of cases. The textual reference is normally related to an epistemic method adopted by the court to evaluate evidence.[288] The Supreme Court of Slovenia refers, instead, to the average person as one of the criteria related to an objective assessment.[289]

In contrast with the Hungarian and Slovenian samples of cases, the English and Italian jurisprudence appear to be dependent on internal criteria of objectivity that are perceived as a manifestation of orthodox epistemic methodology.[290] For instance, in Joseph v Spiller, the court lists the criteria

285 The jury have no right to substitute their own opinion of the literary merits of the work for that of the critic, or to try the 'fairness' of the criticism by any such standard. 'Fair,' therefore, in this collocation certainly does not mean that which the ordinary reasonable man, *'the man on the Clapham omnibus,'* as Lord Bowen phrased it, the juryman common or special, would think a correct appreciation of the work; and it is of the highest importance to the community that the critic should be saved from any such possibility. In principle, therefore, there would be nothing to leave to the jury unless there was some element in the criticism which might support an inference of unfairness in some other sense.' [My emphasis] *Mcquire v Western Morning News Company Limited* (1903) 2 KB 100 (Court of Appeal) 109.

286 MacCormick (n 8).

287 2011-05-04 No. 3K-3-184/2011.

288 N. Bf.104/2006/12.

289 Decision n. II Ips 462/2009.

290 Vito Breda and Mateo Vricella, 'English Pragmatism and Italian Virtue: A Comparative Analysis of the Regime of Illegally Obtained Evidence in Civil Law Proceedings between Italy and England' (2014) 21 Maastricht Journal of European and Comparative Law 428.

that might define objectively fair comments.[291] The counsel for the plaintiff submitted that the respondent had to establish that: 1) the words were used to complain; 2) the comment was on facts; 3) the facts commented on constituted a matter of public interest; 4) the comment was objectively 'fair'; that is, the comment was capable of being honestly founded on the facts to which it related, albeit by someone who was prejudiced and obstinate; and 5) the comment represented the defendant's honest opinion. If he discharged all these burdens, the defence could none the less be defeated by proof of malice on the part of the defendant. However, the UK Supreme Court refused the plaintiff's submission, claiming for itself the right to objectively qualify the type and the range of the respondent's obligations in relation to the case.

A similar internal epistemological methodology was adopted by the Supreme Court of Slovenia in decision n. II Ips 462/2009. The court had to decide over the recognition of a foreign adoption case.[292] One of the questions the court had to answer was whether the effects of such recognition would *objectively be in the child's interest* (Slovenian: *objektivno je/ni v korist otroka*). The best interest of the child was interpreted in the light of internal jurisprudential criteria. The adoption, the court argued, would bring several legal effects that would undoubtedly be in the interest of the child. These effects included all legal consequences stemming from parental rights. A textual analysis of the Slovenian Supreme Court's qualification of an internal concept, that is, the child's best interest, is again a manifestation of the existence of a spectrum of epistemic methods adopted to objectively qualify the court's judicial discretion. The evidence that emerges from our sample of cases suggests that all legal systems rely on internal segmented epistemological structures and that such cognitive methods (e.g. the reasonable person) are considered as one of the necessary requirements for the objective evaluation of legal dilemmas.

291 Spiller v Joseph [2010] UKSC 53.
292 Decision n. II Ips 462/2009.

4. Conclusion

The possibility of an objective judicial decision has inspired a long-lasting debate among both legal practitioners and academics. While it is reasonably clear that a textual reference to objectivity cannot be considered as an apotropaic device to reduce empirical evidence of bias and institutional racism purported by Danziger,[293] the sample of cases considered shows strong indications that courts seek, in the majority of cases, to adopt the best epistemic practice in relation to the issue they have been asked to engage with. Such a result might support Coleman and Leister's idea of the existence of modest objectivity in law. Law, the two authors argue, cannot have a weak claim to objectivity because that might imply that its justification is exclusively internal and thus based on intersubjective assumptions. In addition, a judicial evaluation cannot be exclusively external because legal discourse falls short, for instance, of the stringent criteria set for pure science. In judicial discourse, a modest objectivity might be formulated instead as an attempt to evaluate evidence under an ideal epistemic condition.[294] Given that the circumstances that define the ideal epistemic condition change in relation to the nature of judicial discretion, so do the criteria that have to be used. The study tends to confirm this assumption.

These epistemic methods were divided into three clusters, which I called, respectively, explicit, external and internal segmented epistemology. Each segment represents a spectrum of judicial practices and in a graphical representation, each national legal system has a distinctive third dimension of objective judicial qualification. Again, the results appear to confirm Legrand's idea of national pre-judices.[295] For instance, the textual analysis of a UK Supreme Court jurisprudence shows, by comparison to other legal systems, evidence of a large spectrum of external epistemic methods. Evidence of an explicit segment is perhaps the most interesting aspect of this part of the project. In a limited group of legal systems, the courts decided to describe the epistemic processes adopted in judicial discretion cases and their implications in detail. For instance, in the Slovakian legal

293 Danziger, Levav and Avnaim-Pesso (n 11); Gazal-Ayal and Sulitzeanu-Kenan (n 12).

294 Coleman and Leiter (n 3) 561.

295 Legrand (n 10); Legrand (n 6).

system, judges tended to explain the epistemic method chosen for solving the legal dispute in detail. The reason for making the process explicit is not explained, but it might be part of an attempt to increase the perception of the democratic accountability of the judicial system. This aspect of the study was not explored.

The research, instead, shows the variety of epistemic processes adopted by decisions across areas in which courts had axiomatic discretion. In these cases, the reference to objectivity is not used as a cudgel with which to beat the sceptics and please the sycophants. There are also a few indications of a lackadaisical attitude. For instance, seldom in objective judicial discretion cases is the concept of objectivity referred to as an empty rhetorical concept. The textual analysis of the sample considered in this study indicates, instead, the existence of a cross-cultural judicial commitment to legal objectivity in legal discourse. That commitment is stronger in the debate surrounding complex legal issues where judges have limited discretion.

Bibliography

Alexy R, 'Constitutional Rights, Balancing, and Rationality' (2003) 16 Ratio Juris 131

Azuelos-Atias S, 'Semantically Cued Contextual Implicatures in Legal Texts' (2010) 42 Journal of Pragmatics 728

Bell DA, 'Who's Afraid of Critical Race Theory' [1995] University of Illinois Law Review 893

Boyle J, 'The Politics of Reason: Critical Legal Theory and Local Social Thought' (1985) 133 University of Pennsylvania Law Review 685

Breda V, 'The Grammar of Bias: Judicial Impartiality in European Legal Systems' [2016] International Journal for the Semiotics of Law - First online: 25 July 2016

Breda V and Rodak L (eds), *Diverse Narratives of Legal Objectivity: An Interdisciplinary Perspective* (Peter Lang 2016)

Breda V and Vricella M, 'English Pragmatism and Italian Virtue: A Comparative Analysis of the Regime of Illegally Obtained Evidence in Civil Law Proceedings between Italy and England' (2014) 21 Maastricht Journal of European and Comparative Law 428

Christodoulidis E, *Law and Reflexive Politics* (Kluwer 1998)

Coleman JL and Leiter B, 'Determinacy, Objectivity, and Authority' [1993] University of Pennsylvania Law Review 549

Croce M, 'Precedente Giudiziale E Giurisprudenza Costituzionale' (2006) 4 1114

Danziger S, Levav J and Avnaim-Pesso L, 'Extraneous Factors in Judicial Decisions' (2011) 108 Proceedings of the National Academy of Sciences of the United States of America 6889

Del Mar M, 'The Forward-Looking Requirement of Formal Justice: Neil MacCormick on Consequential Reasoning' (2015) 6 Jurisprudence 429

Delgado R, *Critical Race Theory: An Introduction* (New York University Press 2012)

Douglas G, Pearce J and Woodward H, 'Cohabitants, Property and the Law: A Study of Injustice' (2009) 72 Modern Law Review 24

Douzinas C and Gearey A, *Critical Jurisprudence: The Political Philosophy of Justice* (Hart 2005)

Dworkin R, *Taking Rights Seriously* (Harvard University Press 1978)

_, *A Matter of Principle* (Harvard University Press 1985)

_, *Law's Empire* (Fontana 1986)

Evans N and Levinson SC, 'The Myth of Language Universals: Language Diversity and Its Importance for Cognitive Science' (2009) 32 Behavioral and Brain Sciences 429

Fon V and Parisi F, 'Judicial Precedents in Civil Law Systems: A Dynamic Analysis' (2006) 26 International Review of Law and Economics. 519

Fuller LL, 'Positivism and Fidelity to Law: A Reply to Professor Hart' (1958) 71 Harvard Law Review 630

Gazal-Ayal O and Sulitzeanu-Kenan R, 'Let My People Go: Ethnic In-Group Bias in Judicial Decisions—Evidence from a Randomized Natural Experiment' (2010) 7 Journal of Empirical Legal Studies 403

Goyat S, 'The Basis of Market Segmentation: A Critical Review of Literature' (2011) 3 European Journal of Business and Management 45

Hardt M and Negri A, *Empire* (Harvard University Press 2000)

Hart HLA, 'Positivism and the Separation of Law and Morals' (1958) 71 Harvard Law Review 593

_, *The Concept of Law* (Clarendon Press 1961)

_, *The Concept of Law* (Penelope Bulloch and Joseph Raz eds, Oxford University Press 1997)

Komárek J, 'Reasoning with Previous Decisions: Beyond the Doctrine of Precedent' (2013) 61 American Journal of Comparative Law 149

Kozinski A, 'What I Ate for Breakfast and Other Mysteries of Judicial Decision Making' (1992) 26 Loy. LAL Rev. 993

Lamond G, 'Analogical Reasoning in the Common Law', (2014) Oxford Journal of Legal Studies, Published online first: June 24, 2014

Langacker R, *Foundations of Cognitive Grammar: Volume II: Descriptive Application* (Stanford University Press 1991)

Legrand P, 'European Legal Systems Are Not Converging' (1996) 45 The International and Comparative Law Quarterly 52

_, 'Against a European Civil Code' (1997) 60 The Modern Law Review 44

Levinson SC, *Pragmatics* (Cambridge University Press 1983)

MacCormick N, *Legal Reasoning and Legal Theory* (Clarendon Press 1994)

_, 'Reasonableness and Objectivity' (1998) 74 Notre Dame Law Review 1575

Post R and Rogin MP, *Race and Representation: Affirmative Action* (Zone Books 1998)

Rigaux F, *La Loi Des Juges* (O Jacob 1997)

Rorty R, *Objectivity, Relativism, and Truth* (Cambridge University Press 1991)

Sacco R, 'Legal Formants: A Dynamic Approach to Comparative Law' (1991) 39 The American Journal of Comparative Law 343

Skoczeń I, 'Minimal Semantics and Legal Interpretation' [2015] International Journal for the Semiotics of Law -

Zirk-Sadowski M, 'Interpretation of Law and Judges Communities' (2012) 25 International Journal for the Semiotics of Law - 473

Zucca L, *Constitutional Dilemmas: Conflicts of Fundamental Legal Rights in Europe and the USA* (Oxford University Press 2007)

Chapter 4
A qualitative reflection: objectivity in judicial narratives

1. Introduction

This chapter provides a commentary on the project's results. As mentioned elsewhere in this book, the term *objectivity* refers to a gamut of lexical narratives which are contextually dependant.[296] Judicial objectivity, we found in this project, is no different.[297] The concept of judicial objectivity is deployed by courts with different contextual/functional significances which are related to a series of cognitive significances. These cognitive significances are distinctive of a national community of legal professionals.[298] The research aimed at mapping these functional uses in different legal systems. The project's results are represented in Table 1 (at the end of this chapter). Table 1 (at the end of this chapter) is a simplified representation of the research results extracted by a series of individual research activities. The lexical references to the concept of objectivity are grouped into five macro-groups of textual references called extracts. The table also includes a list of the most common cognitive uses that each legal system associated with an extract. These are the contextual significances that researchers associated

296 Stephen C Levinson, *Pragmatics* (Cambridge University Press 1983); Nicholas Evans and Stephen C Levinson, 'The Myth of Language Universals: Language Diversity and Its Importance for Cognitive Science' (2009) 32 Behavioral and Brain Sciences 429.

297 Pierre Legrand, 'European Legal Systems Are Not Converging' (1996) 45 The International and Comparative Law Quarterly 52; Sol Azuelos-Atias, 'Semantically Cued Contextual Implicatures in Legal Texts' (2010) 42 Journal of Pragmatics 728; Deirdre Wilson and Dan Sperber, 'Relevance Theory' in Laurence R Horn and Gregory L Ward (eds), *The Handbook of Pragmatics* (Blackwell 2006).

298 Jules L Coleman and Brian Leiter, 'Determinacy, Objectivity, and Authority' [1993] University of Pennsylvania Law Review 549; Pierre Legrand, 'Against a European Civil Code' (1997) 60 The Modern Law Review 44.

with the textual references using Langacker's study on grammar and its pragmatic application to judicial decisions.[299]

2. Preliminary notes

The commentary on Table 1 is designed to offer an overview of the results to those who have spent some significant time reading the preceding chapters of this volume.[300] Given the scope and the length of the research material generated by this research, it is expected that some readers, even before reading the introduction, will look to the research results. This chapter will try to cater for both groups of readers. Yet, for those who are not familiar with the role of commentary, it cannot substitute for the specific explanations set out in the preceding chapters of this volume. For those of you who have diligently read the preceding chapters, you might find that some notions will be restated or oversimplified. I apologise in advance for these repetitions.

Before a full explanation of the main results in Table 1 commences, a series of qualifications is necessary. Firstly, the table lists cognitive functional uses of the concept of objectivity by courts in different countries. The term *cognitive function* is connected to a grammatical lexical function of the concept of objectivity and not to an institutional function of the court.[301] The distinction between a lexical analysis and the functional approach is mentioned elsewhere in this volume, but it is important to remember that the aim of this study was to discover the types of judicial contextual uses that we call *cognitive functions* which are associated with the term *objectivity*.[302] This is

299 Ronald Langacker, *Foundations of Cognitive Grammar: Volume II: Descriptive Application* (Stanford University Press 1991); Marek Zirk-Sadowski, 'Interpretation of Law and Judges Communities' (2012) 25 International Journal for the Semiotics of Law - 473; Izabela Skoczeń, 'Minimal Semantics and Legal Interpretation' [2015] International Journal for the Semiotics of Law -; Levinson (n 1).

300 Vito Breda and Lidia Rodak (eds), *Diverse Narratives of Legal Objectivity: An Interdisciplinary Perspective* (Peter Lang 2016); Vito Breda, 'The Grammar of Bias: Judicial Impartiality in European Legal Systems' [2016] International Journal for the Semiotics of Law -.

301 Langacker (n 4); Ronald Langacker, *The Foundations of Cognitive Grammar: Volume I: Theoretical Prerequisites* (Stanford University Press 1999).

302 Azuelos-Atias (n 2); Legrand (n 3).

not a functional approach to comparative studies that assumes all modern democratic legal systems unload similar functions.[303] To begin with, judicial objectivity is not a function of the legal system, rather it is a jurisprudential requirement.[304] For instance, civil procedures should allow a truthful representation of the facts of the case that allow a court to deliver a judgement in both English and Italian courts.[305] A functional approach to comparative law presumed that both systems, in our example, the English and the Italian systems, would have a similar aim and might encounter the same problem. There is rich literature that questions the hermeneutic validity of the functional approach in comparative legal studies,[306] yet this study focuses on the hermeneutic contextual functions of the concept of objectivity.[307]

The project aimed at revealing a cluster of significances of the concept of objectivity. It was not clear, at the start of the study, whether all legal systems had a cluster of references related to the concept of judicial objectivity, or whether each legal system had its own distinctive use of such a concept. There

---

303 The Functional Approach is analysed in a plethora of outlets and it has been used in a series of well reputed studies. See, for instance, these analyses: Mark Tushnet, *Weak Courts, Strong Rights Judicial Review and Social Welfare Rights in Comparative Constitutional Law* (Princeton University Press 2008); Michele Graziadei, 'Legal Transplants and the Frontiers of Legal Knowledge' (2009) 10 Theoretical Inquiries in Law 723; Peter De Cruz, *Comparative Law in a Changing World* (Routledge-Cavendish 2007) 334; Esin Orücü, 'Comparative Law in Practice' in David Nelken and Esin Orücü (eds), *Comparative Law a Handbook.* (Hart 2007); Konrad Zweigert, *Introduction to Comparative Law* (Clarendon Press; Oxford University Press 1998) 34.

304 Coleman and Leiter (n 3); James Boyle, 'The Politics of Reason: Critical Legal Theory and Local Social Thought' (1985) 133 University of Pennsylvania Law Review 685.

305 Vito Breda and Matteo Vricella, 'English Pragmatism and Italian Virtue: A Comparative Analysis of the Regime of Illegally Obtained Evidence in Civil Law Proceedings between Italy and England' (2014) 21 Maastricht journal of European and comparative law 428.

306 Rodolfo Sacco, 'Legal Formants: A Dynamic Approach to Comparative Law' (1991) 39 The American Journal of Comparative Law 343; Helena Whalen-Bridge, 'The Reluctant Comparatist: Teaching Common Law Reasoning to Civil Law Students to Civil Law Students an the Future of Comparative Legal Skills' (2008) 58 Journal of Legal Education; Orücü (n 8).

307 Langacker (n 4).

were, however, strong indications from linguistic studies that suggested the existence of distinctive national cognitive patterns.[308] Evans and Levinson's analysis of meta-cognitive practices tends to support divergence as one of the common dominators in linguistic analyses. Given that judicial reasoning is, at least partially, a semantically based cognitive activity, it was reasonable to speculate that a large multinational analysis would find evidence of nationally diverging cognitive practices.[309]

The answer to the last research question was of particular importance for the judiciary of the European Union (EU) member states, which, in the past thirty years, has been asked to implement the EU treaties and Community Law in a uniform manner. Knowing *how diverse* the lexical understanding of general concepts is across EU judicial systems is also essential for proposed plans such as the one for a constitution for Europe and the one for the European Civil Code.[310] These types of ambitious plans largely depend on the existence of a common understanding of general legal concepts. The study shows that, even at the lexical level, all the legal systems that were considered have unique understandings of general principles such as judicial independence, procedural fairness and justice.

The last preliminary point involves addressing a potential criticism. All legal systems that are designed to respect the rule of law also accept that judicial narratives have to be objective. In other words, if judicial objectivity were a functional element of the rule of law, a study of how courts achieved an objective decision would only be a variation of the comparative functional approach. Yet the aim of the study was to map how courts lexically and cognitively construct the concept of judicial objectivity and not how they evaluate the process adopted to achieve an objective decision. For instance, rhetorical and incongruent uses of the term *objectivity* were considered relevant results because they provided an indication of what is perceived as a meaningful use of the term *objectivity* (and not a failure to deliver the expected institutional function). Similar conclusions are reached

308 Evans and Levinson (n 1); Levinson (n 1) 5.
309 Evans and Levinson (n 1).
310 Legrand (n 3) 50.

in Azuelos-Atias's study of Israeli judicial narratives and in general linguistic analyses.[311]

3. Reading the results of Table 1

In the previous section, we discussed the difference between epistemic functionalism and the functionalist approach to comparative studies.[312] This study is squarely based on an *ad hoc* epistemic functionalism.[313] In this section, we will instead give a short commentary on the graphical representation of the research results. As mentioned earlier, the general outcome was to show acknowledgement of the great disparity of functional uses of the term *objectivity* across the judicial systems that were considered.

In Table 1, the upper row indicates the name of the legal system that was considered. The first column on the left shows the most common textual references to the concept of objectivity. The significances were grouped into five large thematic macro-groups of textual references to the concept of objectivity. These are the macro-groups of extracts. These groups are divided along the lines of general textual significance associated with the concept of judicial objectivity. They include objective interpretation, objectified judicial discretion, objectivity as impartiality, objectivity as truth and objectivity as fairness.

The table should be read by conjoining the textual reference in the text listed within the rows of the first column (called objectivity – lexical references) with the list of cognitive activities in the national columns.

OBJECTIVITY – Lexical references	Brazil	Hungary
Objective interpretation Group A: The text is interpreted objectively because:	Evaluation ↓	Rhetoric ↓
a. the court refers to its literal meaning ================================>	V	V

Example.

311 Azuelos-Atias (n 2) 731; Skoczeń (n 4); Evans and Levinson (n 1).

312 Graziadei (n 8).

313 Azuelos-Atias (n 2); Evans and Levinson (n 1); Levinson (n 1); Langacker (n 4).

For instance, in the table above, the Brazilian sample of cases includes references to objective textual interpretation and that is, in the case of Brazil, normally associated with an evaluation of the possible significances. Similar textual references are seen in the Hungarian sample, but the researchers considered those references as having a rhetorical cognitive function. That is, the court mechanically used the term *objective interpretation* to support its decision but the reference to objectivity is unqualified and it was considered empty of cognitive significance.

These groups of significances, as mentioned in Chapter One, were selected in the early stages of the project. In particular, some of the usages were retrieved by the pilot study conducted by Dr Lidka Rodak at the Silesian University in Katowice, while others were added during the reflexive stages of the project. The objective interpretation group (Table 1) includes all the functional uses of the concept of objectivity that were used by the courts to qualify a textual interpretative activity.[314] This group of textual references and their contextual analysis were discussed in previous publications and they will briefly be discussed in this chapter.[315] Group A might, however, give an indication of the diverging interpretative practices. For instance, the research shows that in interpreting legal documents, Hungarian courts have a general tendency to claim their objective interpretation by making reference to: a literal meaning, the intentions of the legislator, the objective interpretation as performed by the judge and identification with certainty/predictability. Italian courts, instead, tend to associate a claim of objectivity only with interpretative activities carried out by the judge. Again, it is not the aim of the study to explain why Hungarian judges load the output, so to speak, of their interpretation of a text with a range of claims, whereas Italian judges tend to limit the claim of objectivity to their activity (and not to the final result). In addition, it is not the aim of the study to provide a qualitative evaluation of judicial practices which might qualify the Hungarian system as better (or worse) than the Italian one. The project intended to show, instead, how national judicial systems use the concept of objectivity in their jurisprudence.

The second macro-group of extracts is called *objective judicial discretion*. It includes references to the concept of objectivity in cases that seek, for

314 Boyle (n 9).
315 Breda and Rodak (n 5).

instance, to eliminate the arbitrary character of judgements. As explained in Chapter Three, the concept of objectivity is often associated with cases in which the court is asked to evaluate new legal dilemmas or cases that are within the so-called Hartian penumbra. In this typology of cases, in which there is no predetermined explicit legal rule, a range of epistemic methods is used by judges to find the right decision. I called these types of instances *judicial discretion cases*. These decisions are not over a so-called hard case.

> 'On the linear scale that connects hard cases with difficult cases, judicial discretion cases tend to be closer to the former than to the latter. For instance, in judicial discretion cases, the court might be asked to decide which administrative process, from among a number of equivalent processes, might better implement a government policy.'[316]

In judicial discretion cases, by way of comparison to the ones associated with an interpretation of a legal text, judges have a high degree of discretion. Judicial discretion cases are often referred to as examples to support a claim of arbitrariness of judicial decisions.[317] The research found no evidence of arbitrariness, yet the analyses of the Brazilian and Spanish samples of judicial discretion cases show that judges are inclined to use the concept of objectivity rhetorically. That is, without qualifying it or using it in a way that is logically linked with the rest of the decision.[318] These types of hollow functional uses of the concept of objectivity were colloquially designed as 'window-dressing' cognitive devices.

This is a delicate point, so we must be precise. There is no indication that judges in Brazil and Spain acted surreptitiously.[319] The research shows that in instances in which judges have more discretion, they tend to use a

316 Introduction of Chapter 3.3 of this monograph.

317 Oren Gazal-Ayal and Raanan Sulitzeanu-Kenan, 'Let My People Go: Ethnic In-Group Bias in Judicial Decisions—Evidence from a Randomized Natural Experiment' (2010) 7 Journal of Empirical Legal Studies 403; Shai Danziger, Jonathan Levav and Liora Avnaim-Pesso, 'Extraneous Factors in Judicial Decisions' (2011) 108 Proceedings of the National Academy of Sciences of the United States of America 6889.

318 Azuelos-Atias (n 2) 732.

319 Maximiliano Aramburo and Alonso Agüero San Juan Alonso Agüero San Juan, 'Spain: Objectivity in Legal Discourse' <https://eprints.usq.edu.au/> accessed 11 June 2016.

series of epistemic practices. I call them *segmented epistemic practices* because each country defined a specific range of cognitive activities within the larger spectrum of legal reasoning available that is perceived as objective.[320] The lack of consistency between legal systems – some of which are part of the same legal family and have a very similar historical development (such as Spain and Italy) – does not disprove the role of objectivity in cases of judicial discretion.[321] The analysis of the judicial argument from objectivity shows, instead, the existence of a dynamic conception of objectivity which resembles what Coleman and Leiter call *modest objectivity*. In particular, the textual analyses of judicial narratives tend to indicate equanimity and independence in all judicial discretion cases.[322]

At first sight, the results of this part of the analysis are, by way of comparison to the graphical representation of the results of the previous macro-group of significances, less heterogeneous. For instance, the analyses of the Brazilian and Spanish samples of cases deliver the same results. The same might be said for the Hungarian and Slovakian legal systems. In addition, similar results were retrieved from the Italian, Lithuanian and Romanian legal systems.[323]

The third macro-group of functional uses of the concept of objectivity in Table 1 was called the *objectivity impartiality group*, which includes cases in which the concept of objectivity is used by the courts in response to an allegation of bias. The theoretical and pragmatic implications of the concept of objectivity as a qualifier of the requirement for impartiality are discussed in the first chapter of this book. The analysis of our sample shows, for instance, that debates over judicial impartiality engage two distinctive areas of law. The first, which we already mentioned, is a constitutional requirement for political impartiality. The debate over constitutional impartiality is part of diatribes between radical democrats and positivists concerning the interplay of liberalism and judicial narratives. Judges are expected to

320 Perhaps they are part of second order of legal justifications: Neil MacCormick, *Legal Reasoning and Legal Theory* (Clarendon Press 1994) ch 6.

321 Aramburo and Alonso Agüero San Juan (n 24).

322 Coleman and Leiter (n 3).

323 Rūta Kazanavičiūtė, 'Lithuania: Objectivity in Legal Discourse' <https://eprints.usq.edu.au/> accessed 11 June 2016.

decide cases without allowing political views to affect their decisions.[324] This is one of the best-known functional requirements of the rule of law, and as we have seen earlier, it is also one of the most contested. And yet, this study, which focuses on judicial narratives, has found only two cases in a sample of over nine hundred in which a court has been asked to qualify the concept of objectivity.[325] Off course this might not repeal the claim that judges are part of the same Boy's Club.

The objective impartiality group is one of the most articulate. Again, it is not the aim of the study to speculate over the reasons that make the reference to objectivity more articulate by the courts in cases that question the integrity of the court. It is reasonable to expect that courts will refer more often to the concept of judicial objectivity in cases in which the independence of a decision of a lower court is under review and in cases in which the veracity of the evidence provided by the party, such as a witness testimony, is questioned.

Objectivity as truth and objectivity as fairness in Groups D and E, respectively, provide a matrix of cognitive usages associated with the veracity of the judicial decisions. This group includes national samples in which there is no extract with which to compare them against. This is the case, for instance, for the Italian sample of cases. However, the lack of direct textual references is not without significance. Chapter Three includes, for instance, an analysis of the effects of verophobia. That is, according to Taruffo, the fear of truth that distinguishes the Italian system of civil procedures.[326]

4. Uniqueness and odd communalities: commentary on the results

In the previous section, I referred to Table 1, which gives a simplified visual representation of some of the project's research results. On a general level,

---

324 Gary Slapper, *The English Legal System: 2012–2013* (Routledge 2012) 398.

325 Coleman and Leiter (n 3); Coleman and Leiter (n 3); Ronald Dworkin, *Law's Empire* (Hart 1998); Neil MacCormick, 'Reasonableness and Objectivity' (1998) 74 Notre Dame Law Review 1575. Contra, see: Emilios Christodoulidis, *Law and Reflexive Politics* (Kluwer 1998); Zenon Bankowski and Geoff Mungham, *Images of Law* (Routledge & Kegan Paul 1976).

326 Michele Taruffo, 'La Verità Nel Processo' [2012] Rivista Trimestrale di Diritto e Procedura Civile 1117.

Table 1 shows that referencing the concept of judicial objectivity is common for all the national systems considered in this study. However, the textual references to objectivity create a cluster of national meanings and those meanings have a distinctive cognitive use. So the extracts from the Hungarian and the Slovakian samples revealed similar clusters, yet they were associated with different cognitive uses.

a) Objective textual interpretation (Group A)

Group A represents a cluster of references to the concept of objectivity in which judges interpret a legally binding text. That text might be taken from a statutory or binding decision. Group A provides a list of extracts in which courts assert that their chosen interpretation of the text is objective for a series of reasons. The list of reasons was grouped into the following subgroups:

a. That is its literal meaning;
b. That it is the intention of the legislator;
c. That it is coherent with a theory of interpretation;
d. The judge follows an objective methodology;
e. That it is a logical interpretation of the text;
f. All the relevant aspects of the case were considered and the situation is covered by a specific rule; or
g. There is no evidence of bias (the negative definition).

The cluster of reasons is relatively uncontroversial. It is a manifestation of legal positivism, which is the dominant legal philosophy in all the legal systems assessed by this project.[327] For instance, the reference to the principle of a clear rule (Group A, subsection a) as a guarantee of the objectivity of judicial decisions is part of the legal training for common law[328] and for civil law judges.[329] Most of the legal systems make an express reference to

---

327 Aramburo and Alonso Agüero San Juan (n 24); Tilen Štajnpihler and Andrej Kristan, 'Slovenia: Objectivity in Legal Discourse' <https://eprints.usq.edu.au/> accessed 11 June 2016.

328 HLA Hart, *The Concept of Law* (Clarendon Press 1961) ch 4.

329 H Patrick Glenn, *Legal Traditions of the World: Sustainable Diversity in Law* (Oxford University Press 2010) ch 5.

the purpose of the legislator (Group A, subsection b), which again is one of the orthodoxies purported by legal positivism.

However, the role that these textual references play in a contextual reading of the case based on a cognitive grammatical analysis is distinctive of each legal system. In the majority of the cases considered in the Hungarian sample, for instance, a contextual analysis of these references shows that they are inserted in the decision to provide a description, an evaluation, or for rhetorical effect. These three cognitive usages are distinctive of the Hungarian judicial discourse, and the matrix (i.e. the intersection between textual references and the variation in their cognitive use) is distinctive of that legal system. Indeed, asserting that a rule is interpreted literally might not, at the same time, have the function to describe, to evaluate, or to provide rhetorical support for a decision. The function of evaluating a rule in an objective way is antithetical to making a rhetorical reference to a perhaps irrelevant legal text. However, the aim of the study was not to show which legal system makes more use of the concept of objectivity, but how the clusters of those references compare. So, in the case of the Hungarian judicial sample, there is evidence of the largest, by way of comparison to the other legal systems considered in this study, cluster of references to the concept of objectivity (Group A, subsections a–d and f). Yet, the cognitive use of the references is normally limited to a description, an evaluation of the applicability of the rule, or it has a mere rhetorical effect. The Spanish cluster of textual references to the concept of objectivity is, by way of comparison to the Hungarian cluster, limited. The cognitive uses of the reference, however, include descriptions, evaluations, or explanations.

The matrix formed by the intersection of Group A and the national function does not provide a narrative that supports qualitative differences between the two legal systems. The matrix gives an indication of the distinctive approach that a national judicial system might have to interpreting a legal text. These results confirm, again, the hypothesis that legal systems tend to adopt a modest conception of judicial objectivity,[330] and that that conception is also distinctive of each legal system.[331]

330 Coleman and Leiter (n 3).

331 Nicholas Aroney and James Allan, 'An Uncommon Court: How the High Court of Australia Has Undermined Australian Federalism' (2008) 30 Sydney Law Review 245.

b) Objectified judicial discretion (Group B)

In the analysis of the cases represented in Group B of the table, the court has objective judicial discretion but it argues that its decisions remain objective. These are the cases in which, for instance, there is a factual situation that is not covered by legislation (e.g. a case of e-commerce that might result in tax avoidance). Cases of objective judicial discretion also involved the evaluation of expert technical witnesses who might have discordant answers over the same technical dilemma. Again, the court, in the case of discordant expert reports, has the prerogative to accommodate different technical narratives. So Group B included cases in which the court has discretion, yet it makes a textual reference to the concept of objectivity to explain that such discretion is limited.

The sample of cases revealed three types of extracts. Firstly, the courts might refer to a professional report to reduce the subjective character of a decision. The reference to external sources is an important methodological step since it includes an implicit admission that a legalist reading of norms is not sufficient to decide a case. Secondly, the court might sanction the epistemological process that they have used to decide as objective without further explanation. These types of narratives are squarely self-referential and part of a tendency to use the concept of objectivity as a rhetorical cognitive device. Thirdly, the courts referred to academic studies and explicitly declared such studies as objective limitations to the court's discretion. This is a reasoned qualification of the objective discretion of the court, which is, from an epistemological perspective, the most interesting because the reasons provided will affect future decisions. 'It is a relatively common mistake to assume that the doctrine of stare decisis radically differentiates the civil and common law systems.[332] Civil judges are also obliged to provide consistent decisions (the so-called horizontal effect of the doctrine of the binding precedent) and to comply with the case law of the final appellate jurisdictions (the so-called vertical effect) of the final appellate decisions.'[333]

---

332 See J. Komárek, 'Reasoning with Previous Decisions: Beyond the Doctrine of Precedent', 61 *American Journal of Comparative Law* (2013), 149–171, 149, 160–167, 170.

333 See V. Fon and F. Parisi, 'Judicial Precedents in Civil Law Systems: A dynamic Analysis', 26 *International Review of Law and Economics* (2006), 519–535;

This point is well engaged in Parglender. He explained that separating common law and civil law systems along the line set by the doctrine of the binding precedent is misleading.[334]

An analysis of the sample shows that academic writing does influence judicial decisions. In the majority of the legal systems considered in this study, judges, who have to decide a case in which there is no clear answer and for which they have some discretion, made references to academic studies. Group B, subsection a, shows that judges in hard cases seek inspiration outside the legal system. It is important to remember that researchers had to find textual references to such an activity in the text. For instance, references to an academic opinion that was not attributed to a specific author were not considered. Once the textual reference to an academic or professional study was inserted in the case, each legal system associated the reference with a distinctive cognitive activity. For instance, only Slovenian and Brazilian courts associated a reference to academic writings with an evaluation of the significance that such a text might have on qualifying the concept of judicial objectivity. Judges, in the other legal systems considered in this study, might refer to academic analyses for rhetorical reasons.[335] I could continue with the analysis of Group B, but this group of textual qualifications of the concept of objectivity confirms the uniqueness of national pre-judices. Group B might also give an indication of a lack of convergence of judicial narratives among former communist legal systems.[336] For instance, in cases where the objective discretion was placed in the hands of judges, the Hungarian and Slovakian decisions might appear to have adopted a similar textual syntax (Group B, subsections a and b),[337] yet a contextual analysis suggests that Hungarian judges tend to use such studies in a way that favours empty descriptions

---

M. Croce, 'Precedente Giudiziale e Giurisprudenza Costituzionale', 4–5 *Contratto e Impresa* (2006), 1114–1161; R. Sacco, 'Legal Formants: A Dynamic Approach to Comparative Law', 39 *The American Journal of Comparative* Breda and Vricella (n 10). *Law* (1991), 343–401, 356.

334 See, for a critical review of the concept of legal family, M. Pargendler, 'The Rise and Decline of Legal Families', 60 *American Journal of Comparative Law* (2012), 1043–1074.

335 Aramburo and Alonso Agüero San Juan (n 24); Štajnpihler and Kristan (n 32).

336 Legrand (n 3) 51.

337 Langacker (n 4).

(perhaps by reporting one of the parties' submissions) or as a rhetorical device (to support a subjective decision). The data from the Hungarian and Slovenian samples shows that both judicial systems refer to the activity of the court as objective (Group B, subsection b), yet in the case of the Slovakian sample, there are also reasonable indications of an attempt to explain the epistemic reasons (by evaluating, for instance, the effects of such a choice) of such a decision.

c) Objective impartiality (Group C)

Macro-Group C includes extracts from cases in which the concept of objectivity has been coupled with a qualification of judicial bias. These samples of cases are appeal proceedings against a standing decision or preliminary rulings which seek to alter the composition of the court. The Pinochet Ugarte n. 2 is one of the best-known examples of an appeal decision against a previous decision.[338] As for the rest of this study, macro-Group C was divided into different subgroups associated with specific textual references to the concept of objectivity. These subgroups are:

a. The court refers to the subjective impartiality of the judge;
b. The court refers to the objective impartiality of the judge;
c. The court refers to external objective criteria;
d. The court references the activity of a third party (subjective bias);
e. The court's decision is de facto unbiased;
f. The court's decision considered all the facts of the case;
g. The court refers to the opinion of experts; or
h. The court refers to legal rules and procedures.

As mentioned earlier, negative variations, in which the court defined what could not be associated with the concept of objectivity, were considered as false positives. Table 1 – Group C, subsections c, e, f and g are mostly found in cases in which a party alleges an objective interest of the judge in the

338 Kerry Abadee, 'Lessons from the Pinochet Case for the Bias Rule of Procedural Fairness in Its Application to Australian Judges' 8 Journals, Australian Journal of Administrative Law 19; *R v Bow Street Metropolitan Stipendiary Magistrate Ex p Pinochet Ugarte (No2) [2000]* (1999) 1 AC 119 (HL).

decision. For instance, the judge is a shareholder of one of the companies that is a party to the case in which s/he is called to decide.

Subgroup f (within macro-Group C) is the only type of textual reference that is found in all the legal systems considered in this study. This is one of the most interesting results of the study because it gives an indication of the shared role of strong epistemic methods in judicial narratives. Coleman and Leiter qualify the categories of strong, modest and weak objectivity in judicial reasoning.[339] A strong metaphysic (which, as discussed in Chapter One, is not without its critiques) tends to be found in natural science.[340] It is a distinctive form of epistemic reasoning that is not based on individual or group perceptions and tends to be linked with objective truth-finding inquiries. Results based on a strong metaphysic require, for instance, reproducibility and independent validation and they are common in engineering. Judicial reasoning relies, however, on modest objectivity that combines strong epistemic methods associated with factual narrative and textual interpretation.[341] It is for this reason that the extracts represented in *subgroup f* might provide the most important results of this project. In particular, Table 1 shows that all legal systems considered factual narratives as essential epistemological elements in evaluating an allegation of bias.

Furthermore, by comparing the extract with the cognitive significance that each legal system has adopted (i.e. the intersection of Table 1 – Group C, subsections c, e and f), it is reasonable to suggest that there are no significant differences between the clusters of cognitive activities in all the legal systems considered in this study. There are minor variations. For instance, the Slovakian sample reported the largest cluster of significances. It is also worth mentioning that the Slovakian, Slovenian, Romanian and British samples also show a relatively large spectrum of cognitive activities associated with a qualification of judicial objectivity. The Brazilian, the Italian and the

339 Coleman and Leiter (n 3) 559.

340 Georg Wilhelm Friedrich Hegel, *Phenomenology of Spirit* (JN Findlay ed, Oxford University Press 1979); John Skorupski and Crispin Wright, 'Realism, Meaning and Truth' (1988) 38 The Philosophical Quarterly 500; Coleman and Leiter (n 3) 608.

341 Peter J Coleman, 'Review of New Zealand Aspirations in the Pacific in the Nineteenth Century' (1965) 37 The Journal of Modern History 382, 612.

Hungarian samples yielded a smaller cluster of extracts and, perhaps as a consequence of that, a small group of cognitive activities.

As for the rest of this study, the reason for similar or diverging clusters is a matter of speculation. It would be possible to speculate, for instance, that there is a linear connection between legal systems that shared a chain of common geopolitical borders. In addition, Slovakia, Slovenia and Hungary were parts of the Austro-Hungarian Empire.[342] There are, however, speculative narratives that might require a further analysis. Similar conclusions might be deduced from an analysis of the Spanish legal system. Historically, Spain has, like Hungary, Slovakia and Slovenia, experienced a long period of dictatorship, yet Spanish judges seldom refer to the concept of judicial objectivity as a qualifier of judicial bias.

Table 1 – Group C, subgroups a, d and h correspond to extracts that were principally associated with a qualification of subjective judicial bias. An allegation of subjective bias, by way of comparison to an allegation of objective judicial bias, suggests a personal connection between one of the judges and one of the parties. The extracts taken from these types of cases were divided into three groups:

a. The court refers to the subjective impartiality of the judge;
d. The court references the activity of a third party (subjective bias); or
h. The court's decision references legal rules and procedures.

The matrix formed by the extracts and their relative contextual epistemic practices suggests that allegations of subjective judicial bias are a proxy for a large variation in narratives.

For instance, the analysis of the Hungarian sample shows that allegations of judicial bias are coupled with an objective description of the relationship between the judge and one of the parties. The Slovakian sample of cases shows that courts tend to link an allegation of subjective judicial bias with a description of the claim, an evaluation of its persuasiveness and an assessment of its effect on the decision.[343] In the British legal system, instead, allegations of judicial bias (Group C, subgroup a) trigger an evaluation of

342 Eric Hobsbawm, *Nations and Nationalism since 1780: Programme, Myth, Reality* (Cambridge University Press 1992) 194.
343 IV. ÚS 38/09, IV. ÚS 303/2010.

the plausibility of the perception of bias.[344] In the UK, the quality of the motivation purported by the court to support its decision or the respect of the requirement of procedural justice is not part of the evaluation of judicial bias. The jurisprudence of the House of Lords (the current UK Supreme Court) shows that a reasonable person should have to perceive one of the judges of the case as biased.[345] Spain and Slovenia share a similar set of contextual epistemic practices.[346]

It is important to mention that extracts associated with Group C, subgroups d, f and h, should also be considered a manifestation of an analysis of factual narratives. The extract taken from the samples often refers to a relation which had to be factually proven, such as a romantic relation between a judge and one of the parties, which had to be proved by objectively retrieved evidence. The textual references included in Group C, subgroup f (*the decision considered all the facts of the case*) are used to qualify allegations of objective and subjective bias. For instance, an allegation of objective bias requires a factual analysis that proves a direct interest of a judge in a dispute. An analysis of the evidence is also essential on the cognitive activity aimed at verifying the plausibility of an allegation of a pre-existing relation between the court and one of the parties (e.g. the judge and one of the parties share the same residence).

Furthermore, the reference to a third party (Group C, subgroup d) might be a reference to a witness. The evolution of the persuasiveness of external accounts might be measured against general concepts such as the reasonable person. These legal criteria have the effect of displacing the debate over whether the judge has been de facto biased in the decision, to a debate over *potential* pernicious effects of a personal relation between the judge and one of the parties.

At the start of the project, it was expected that both objective and subjective allegations of bias would have generated a large variation in extracts. The level of complexity and variations in the correlation between abstracts

---

344 *R. v Bow Street Metropolitan Stipendiary Magistrate Ex p. Pinochet Ugarte (No. 2) [2000]* (n 43).

345 *R. v Bow Street Metropolitan Stipendiary Magistrate Ex p. Pinochet Ugarte (No. 2) [2000]* (n 43); Abadee (n 43).

346 Aramburo and Alonso Agüero San Juan (n 24); Štajnpihler and Kristan (n 32).

and pre-judices is, however, almost mindboggling. The spectrum of variations has pragmatic implications. So there are instances in which the procedural soundness of the trial might be used to repeal an allegation of bias. Evidence of such epistemic methodology is found in the Slovenian and Lithuanian legal systems. In the UK, evidence of a reasonable connection between the party and a judge is sufficient to justify a retrial or a change of the judicial panel. These are not indications of the level of impartiality of a judicial system. The intention of the study was to indicate how allegations of bias are decided on the basis of national pre-judices and data shows a strong indication that, in cases of an allegation of judicial bias, each national system relies on a cluster of narratives and these narratives are coupled with a substantial variation in judicial cognitive activities.

d) Objectivity as truth (Group D)

The relations between judicial objectivity and the concept of truth are discussed in the second chapter of this book and Group D provides a graphic representation of the project's results. On a general level, Group D confirms the existence of national clusters of the interplay between the concept of objectivity and truth which support the existence of Legrand's idea of pre-judices.[347] The role of truth in legal reasoning is deeply contested, but the aim of the study was not to find out whether courts function as truth-finding institutions or which legal system was better at achieving such an aim.[348] This part of the project aimed instead at mapping out how courts qualify the connecting concept of judicial objectivity *and* truth.[349] The extracts were divided into five subgroups. The court asserts that its analysis is objectively truthful because:

---

347 Legrand (n 2) 51.

348 Skorupski and Wright (n 45); Richard Rorty, *Richard Rorty: Philosophical Papers Set: Objectivity, Relativism, and Truth (Philosophical Papers, Vol. 1): Volume 1* (Cambridge University Press 1990); Richard Uviller, 'Advocate, the Truth, and Judicial Hackles: A Reaction to Judge Frankel's Idea' (1975) 123 University of Pennsylvania Law Review 1067.

349 Ronald Dworkin, *Law's Empire* (Fontana 1986) 76.

a. the court refers to facts;
b. the court refers to expert witnesses;
c. the court refers to a truthful interpretation of a legal text;
d. the parties agree on the issue; or
e. it is procedurally accurate.

As for the rest of the data represented in Table 1, the extracts are textual references that are to be interpreted in relation to the most common cognitive uses by each of the national systems considered in this study.

A quick scan of Group D shows that the Brazilian and the Italian samples of cases do not include a single reference to the concept of truth and justice. This lacuna might support Taruffo's idea of procedural verophobia in the Italian legal system.[350] Taruffo explains that Italian civil procedures are dominated by strict formalism which gives priority to outward appearances of legality at the expense of truth. He uses the term *verophobes* to describe the supporters of strict formalism in the Italian legal system. So, the sample might show evidence of verophobia. The reason for the lack of extracts in the Brazilian sample of cases is not discussed in depth in this book.[351]

The Italian and the Brazilian samples did not include references to truth and justice. Table 1 shows national similarities in the rest of the matrix. For instance, in all legal systems (except for the Italian and Brazilian systems), judges make a direct connection between facts, judicial objectivity and truth. The shared assumption of a connection between facts appears to confirm Leiter and Coleman's strong metaphysical assumptions in factual narratives.[352] Judicial decisions do depend on scientific evidence (e.g. DNA reports) and, it is logical to assume, that the judicial contextual analyses related to that evidence are a manifestation of the scientific method. It is important to note that the UK sample of cases includes indirect references to

350 Taruffo (n 31).
351 Yves-Andre Faure, 'Jeitinho and Other Related Phenomena in Contemporary Brazil' in Daniel Bach and Mamoudou Gazibo (eds), *Neopatrimonialism in Africa and Beyond* (Routledge 2013); Mario Caciagli, 'The Long Life of Clientelism in Southern Italy' in Jun'ichi Kawata (ed), *Comparing political corruption and clientelism* (Ashgate 2006); Junichi Kawata (ed), *Comparing Political Corruption And Clientelism* (Ashgate 2006).
352 Coleman and Leiter (n 3).

the concept of objective truth but they are taken from libel cases where the parties seek a qualification of the truth to avoid or to impose a liability.[353]

e) Objectivity as fairness (Group E)

The last group of extracts in Table 1 considers the qualification of the concept of judicial objectivity as fairness or justice. The interrelation between judicial objectivity and fairness/justice has yielded the least amount of textual references. The Slovenian sample of cases included ten semantic extracts, Romania three, Hungary, Lithuania and Italy one each, and Brazil and Spain none. The UK sample included over thirteen series of mainly indirect references to judicial objectivity as fairness.

As suggested for the other groups of extracts, the most general indication from Group E is the existence of multiple national clusters of cognitive uses of the concept of judicial objectivity. The result confirms Legrand's suggestion that judges do make decisions on the basis of pre-judices that are a manifestation of a distinctive legal culture.[354] In particular, the interplay between fairness and justice shows a distinctive British pendant for associating the concept of fairness with the idea of judicial objectivity. This is not surprising. The concept of fairness has been one of the key features of modern Anglo-Saxon political theory.[355] The idea of fairness as underpinning an equitable distribution of resources in liberal society is, however, different from the one adopted in the sample. In the majority of the British cases, the concept of fairness is associated with a distribution of resources between the parties such

353 Uviller (n 53).

354 Legrand (n 3); Glenn (n 34).

355 Abadee (n 43); David Estlund, 'Beyond Fairness and Deliberation' in James Bohman and William Rehg (eds), *Deliberative democracy: essays on reason and politics* (MIT 1997); Abadee (n 43); John Rawls, '"Justice as Fairness: Political Not Metaphysical", Philosophy and Public Affairs, 14 (3), Summer, 223-51' (1998) 97 International Library of Critical Writings in Economics 250; GJ Syme, BE Nancarrow and JA McCreddin, 'Defining the Components of Fairness in the Allocation of Water to Environmental and Human Uses' (1999) 57 Journal of Environmental Management 51; John Rawls, *Political Liberalism* (Columbia University Press 2005); John Rawls, 'The Idea of Public Reason' in William Rehg (ed), *Deliberative Democracy: Essays on Reason and Politics* (MIT 1997).

as the husband and wife during a divorce. The reference to fairness is also associated with the compliance (or the lack of it) with procedures. The idea of fairness as a procedural requirement and its interplay with judicial objectivity is found in the UK and Slovenian samples of cases. As mentioned earlier in this book, the higher number of references to fairness is not a qualitative indication of the legal systems considered in Group E. The distinctiveness of the UK sample might simply be due to sociological practices.[356] In other words, there is no indication that English, Northern Irish, Welsh, and Scottish judges are more concerned with the fairness of their decisions or indeed with the fairness of their society.

5. Some Final Comments

Judicial objectivity is perceived as one the cornerstones of all the legal systems considered in this study. This chapter provides a commentary on Table 1, which gives a visual representation of the results of this study.

On a general level, the research shows that each legal system that was considered is unique. Each sample of decisions (over one hundred per legal system) yielded a cluster of lexical references to judicial objectivity.[357] This extract generated a 'matrix' of cognitive uses. So, for instance, the reference to objective expert witness reports might be associated with an evaluation of one of the parties' claims. The intersection of the textual reference with the most common cognitive uses generated a national matrix that, like a DNA structure, distinguishes each of the legal systems considered by this study. Indeed, some legal systems share some lexical qualifications of the concept of objectivity and they might also partake of the cognitive implications, which might be the case in the Hungarian and Slovakian legal systems, but it is reasonably clear that each legal national jurisprudence has a unique understanding of the idea of judicial objectivity. The unique matrix of textual references and cognitive usages, which Legrand calls pre-judices, might have been the result of a natural selection of epistemic methodologies in law.[358] While it is reasonable to suggest pre-judices have developed via a

356 Glenn (n 34) 257.
357 Langacker (n 6); Levinson (n 1); Breda (n 5); Skoczeń (n 4).
358 Peter Stein, *Legal Evolution: The Story of an Idea* (Cambridge University Press 2009) ch 4.

process of logical selection of the best legal qualification of judicial objectivity, the study was not designed to detect stages of historical evolution. Following the same reasoning, the study does not provide a narrative that voids historical evaluations of legal systems.[359] The aim of the study was instead to show whether multiple judicial systems adopt a similar concept of judicial objectivity. The short answer to the question is in the negative.

The concept of objectivity that emerged from the analysis of over thousand cases from nine legal systems is a multifaceted, culturally dependent complex vessel of cognitive activities. These cognitive activities are manifested in a cluster of textual references. The textual references to objectivity do not include an evolution of the so-called co-text. This point is discussed in the introduction, but the co-text could be defined as the information that a group of individuals, such as legal professionals and legal scholars, share as part of their common legal knowledge.[360] The first column of Table 1 gives an indication of the richness of textual references that courts have used to qualify the concept of objectivity. The intersection between the textual references and the list of national legal systems shows that each judicial system tends to have its preferred set of textual qualifications of the concept of objectify. These are instances in which a court makes a reference to the concept of objectivity to qualify its decision. The textual references, however, might not give an indication of the actual cognitive activity associated with the concept of objectivity. It is for this reason that textual references were also evaluated in relation to their distinctive cognitive function. In this part of the project, the researchers assessed the actual cognitive use by the court of the textual reference to objectivity. The 'veil of ignorance', so to speak, that covered the classification of the textual reference was removed and the researchers selected the most common cognitive activities associated with the textual reference.[361] The result is a national matrix of cognitive uses that change in relation to the type of textual references and in relation

359 Stein (n 63); Mathias Reimann, 'The Historical School against Codification: Savigny, Carter, and the Defeat of the New York Civil Code' (1989) 37 The American Journal of Comparative Law 95.

360 Skoczeń (n 4) 2–3; Evans and Levinson (n 1).

361 Breda (n 5); Skoczeń (n 4); Levinson (n 1); Umberto Eco, *Semiotics and the Philosophy of Language* (Indiana University Press 1986).

to the object of adjudication. For instance, textual references to objectivity and truth might be used as rhetorical devices in British libel cases or indicate an evaluation of the facts in Lithuanian administrative decisions.

The main results of the study are depicted in Table 1. The table sheds some light on the debates over the dominant descriptive theories of adjudication. For instance, Hart's criticism of legal realism as an unattainable theory of adjudication is largely unsupported by this study.[362] The study purports strong indications that cognitive processes associated with the concept of judicial objectivity are based on national perceptions that are reproduced, for whatever reason, in daily practices. So, multinational statutory measures, such as EU regulations, are highly unlikely to produce similar effects in different legal systems.[363] The section regarding what is perceived as the best cognitive method by a judicial system is, for the realists and some positivists, notably MacCormick, based on a perception of the social advantage that it might bring to that particular area of law.[364] MacCormick, for instance, postulated that judges do evaluate the pragmatic and legal consequences of their judicial decisions.[365]

The study shows, instead, that each judicial system considered in this book extensively relies on pre-judices and that a range of epistemic methods defines what is perceived as an objective judicial discourse. These sets of epistemic methods are consistently referred to within a legal system and, we can assume, such a practice delivers reasonably reliable judicial decisions.[366] Again, the study indicates that judges are members of a sociological group and the epistemic methods are perceived as appropriate.[367] This finding is particularly evident in cases in which there is an allegation of objective judicial bias and the court refers to external objective criteria. That is, Group C, subgroup c of Table 1. The reference to scientific external criteria, such as

---

362 Hart (n 33) 65–66.

363 Coleman and Leiter (n 3) 567.

364 E Hunter Taylor, 'H. L. A. Hart's Concept of Law in the Perspective of American Legal Realism' (1972) 35 The Modern Law Review 606, 611; MacCormick, 'Reasonableness and Objectivity' (n 30).

365 Neil MacCormick, *Rhetoric and The Rule of Law: A Theory of Legal Reasoning* (Oxford University Press 2005) ch 6; Breda and Vricella (n 10).

366 Coleman and Leiter (n 3) 560.

367 Legrand (n 3).

the one adopted by the forensic accountant that proved a vested interest of a judge in the case that s/he was called to decide,[368] is the only group of extracts that has been found in all the national samples considered by this study. Similar considerations can be made for the references to an expert or an academic (Group B, subgroup a) in cases in which the court has objective judicial discretion.[369] These are instances in which judges are asked to decide a case in which there is no clear rule and where at least one of the parties submits evidence taken from an expert witness. Cases of judicial discretion are often mentioned to support a critique of indeterminacy in law[370]; it is, therefore, quite important for courts to adopt methodologies that are perceived as objective and in tune with legal principles that underpin that legal system.[371]

The popularity of judicial references to scientific and expert reports is, again, coherent with Coleman and Leiter's idea of modest objectivity in law. The idea of modest objectivity in law suggests that multiple judicial epistemic methods are considered as adequate to solve a legal dilemma. However, the court decision to opt for a set of distinctive epistemic methods (and the effect of that judicial decision) have to be within a range that is perceived as objective by the national community of legal practitioners. The existence of a range of possible outcomes does not signify that such a legal system is biased. There is little, or no evidence of the ideological colonisation of judicial discourse. Only on two occasions, in over a thousand cases, did two different courts have to deal with a claim of political bias. Coleman and Leiter's dismissal of the Critical Legal Studies movement appears supported by the results of the study reported in this book.[372] Judges might manifest national variations and linguistic preferences in their

368 Anthony A Owojori and TO Asaolu, 'The Role of Forensic Accounting in Solving the Vexed Problem of Corporate World' (2009) 29 European Journal of Scientific Research 183.

369 Breda (n 5).

370 Dworkin (n 54) 87.

371 Coleman and Leiter (n 3) 549; Boyle (n 9) 695.

372 Brian Leiter, 'Law and Objectivity' in Jules L Coleman, Scott Shapiro and KE Himma (eds), *The Oxford Handbook of Jurisprudence and Philosophy of Law* (Oxford University Press 2004).

decisions, but these variations are not associated with a particular liberal (or capitalist) ideology.

It is also reasonable to suggest that coupling the concept of judicial objectivity with an abstract idea, such as MacCormick's 'reasonable person', might not give a fair presentation of how objectivity is constructed by courts.[373] Intersubjective references are used but not as often as MacCormick suggested. On a more general level, judges seldom provide definitions of general terms. Our research confirmed that judges tend to skirt around the need for a definition of objectivity. It is far more common to find, in our sample, a lexical qualification that explains the function of the concept of objectivity by, for instance, making reference to procedural fairness or to the independence of expert witnesses.

There are pragmatic implications of having a gamut of significances connected to the concept of judicial objectivity. For instance, it could be argued that large legal homogenisation processes, such as the one required by the EU, should consider the judicial implications of the plurality of significances of general terms such as judicial objectivity, judicial independence and justice.[374] Legrand delivers a powerful argument against the idea of a European Civil Code. He argues that legal systems are sociological entities which operate by using a set of implicit 'pre-understandings. They are the manifestations of a professional identity that reacts in a distinctive way, not necessarily negatively, to processes of the homogenisation and convergence of legal systems.[375] Similar concerns should be raised, according to this study, for all transnational statutory measures.

---

373 MacCormick, 'Reasonableness and Objectivity' (n 30).

374 Legrand (n 2); Legrand (n 3).

375 Glenn (n 34) 2.

Table 1[376]

OBJECTIVITY - Extracts	COGNITIVE FUNCTIONS								
	Brazil	Hungary	Italy	Lithuania	Romania	Slovakia	Slovenia	Spain	UK
Objective interpretation GROUP A: THE TEXT is interpreted objectively because:	Evaluation	Description; Evaluation; Rhetoric,	Evaluation	Correctness and validity	Evaluation 2	Evaluation; Correctness and Validity	Rhetoric	Description; Evaluation; Correctness and validity; Rethoric,	Description; Evaluation; Rhetoric, 2
a. the court refers to its literal meaning	V	V		V					V
b. the court refers to the intentions of the legislator		V		V			V	V	V
c. the court refers to a coherent theory of interpretation		V							
d. the court refers to an objective activity of interpretation	V	V	V			V			
e. the court refers to a logical and therefore an objective interpretation									V
f. the court refers to an holistic interpretation that support an objective judicial interpretation		V							
g. there are no evidence of bias (the negative definition)					V	V		V	
Objective judicial discretion GROUP B: The Court has an OBJECTIVE JUDICIAL DISCRETION but its decision remains objective because:	Evaluation	Description; Evaluation; Rhetoric,	Evaluation; Procedural Correctness and Validity; Rhetoric,	Evaluation; Rhetoric,	Rhetoric, Correctness	Description, Evaluation; Procedural Correctness; Rhetoric,	Evaluation	Description; Evaluation	Performative function
a. the court references to academic/professional studies to reduce the subjective character of a decision	V	V	V			V	V	V	
b. the court decides that its activity is objective		V		V	V	V			V
c. the court mixed narratives from the point a. and b.	V							V	
Objective Impartiality GROUP C: The Court is engaging an ALLEGATION OF BIAS but its decision is objective because:	Evaluation	Evaluation,	Evaluation; Rhetoric,	Evaluation; Rhetoric,	Evaluation;	Description; Evaluation; Procedural Correctness and validity	Correctness and validity, Description, Evaluation, Procedural Rhetoric,	Description, Evaluation, Correctness and Validity	Description; Evaluation;
a. the court refers to the subjective impartiality of the judge		V				V			V
b. the court refers to the objective impartiality of the judge					V	V	V		
c. the court refers to external objective criteria,	V	V	V	V	V	V		V	V
d. the court references the activity of a third party (subjective bias)		V		V		V	V		V
e. the court' s decision is de facto unbiased		V	V		V	V	V	V	
f. the court' s decision considered all the facts of the case	V	V	V	V	V	V	V	V	V
g. the court' s decision referred to the opinion of experts	V		V	V		V		V	V
h. the court' s decision references legal rules and procedures			V		V	V			
Objectivity as truth GROUP D: The court asserts that its analysis is objectively TRUTHFUL because	No extracts	Evaluation, Rhetorical	No extracts	Evaluation	Description, Evaluation,	Evaluation,	Description ,Correctness and Validity	Description, Evaluation	Rhetorical , Description
a. the court refer to facts (that are objectively retrieved)		V		V	V	V	V	V	V
b. the court refers to expert witnesses						V			
c. the court refers to a truthful interpretation of legal text								V	
c. the parties agree on the issue		V		V			V		V
d. it is procedurally accurate		V				V			
Objectivity as fairness GROUP E: The court asserts that its decision is objectively FAIR or JUST because	No extracts	Description	Description	Description	Description, Evaluation	Description, Evaluation, Rethorical	Evaluation	No Extracts	Evaluation
a. the court applies a rule		V	V	V	V	V	V		V
b. the court considered an argument sufficiently justified		V			V	V			V
c. the process is correct (e.g. transparent, balanced)				V	V	V	V		V
d. the court evaluate the transfer of rights		V				V	V		V

376 The project's raw data is available for review via the Australia's Academic and Research Network (AARNet).

Bibliography*

Abadee K, 'Lessons from the Pinochet Case for the Bias Rule of Procedural Fairness in Its Application to Australian Judges' 8 Journals, Australian Journal of Administrative Law 19

Aramburo M and Alonso Agüero San Juan AASJ, 'Spain: Objectivity in Legal Discourse' 'Australia's Academic and Research Network' <https://www.aarnet.edu.au> accessed 13 August 2016

Aroney N and Allan J, 'An Uncommon Court: How the High Court of Australia Has Undermined Australian Federalism' (2008) 30 Sydney Law Review 245

Azuelos-Atias S, 'Semantically Cued Contextual Implicatures in Legal Texts' (2010) 42 Journal of Pragmatics 728

Bankowski Z and Mungham G, *Images of Law* (Routledge & Kegan Paul 1976)

Boyle J, 'The Politics of Reason: Critical Legal Theory and Local Social Thought' (1985) 133 University of Pennsylvania Law Review 685

Breda V, 'The Grammar of Bias: Judicial Impartiality in European Legal Systems' [2016] International Journal for the Semiotics of Law - First online: 25 July 2016

Breda V and Rodak L (eds), *Diverse Narratives of Legal Objectivity: An Interdisciplinary Perspective* (Peter Lang 2016)

Breda V and Vricella M, 'English Pragmatism and Italian Virtue: A Comparative Analysis of the Regime of Illegally Obtained Evidence in Civil Law Proceedings between Italy and England' (2014) 21 Maastricht Journal of European and Comparative Law 428

Caciagli M, 'The Long Life of Clientelism in Southern Italy' in Jun'ichi Kawata (ed), *Comparing political corruption and clientelism* (Ashgate 2006)

Christodoulidis E, *Law and Reflexive Politics* (Kluwer 1998)

Coleman JL and Leiter B, 'Determinacy, Objectivity, and Authority' [1993] University of Pennsylvania Law Review 549

Coleman PJ, 'Review of New Zealand Aspirations in the Pacific in the Nineteenth Century' (1965) 37 The Journal of Modern History 382

---

* Please note that Case Law and Statutes are available via Australia's Academic and Research Network (AARNet).

Danziger S, Levav J and Avnaim-Pesso L, 'Extraneous Factors in Judicial Decisions' (2011) 108 Proceedings of the National Academy of Sciences of the United States of America 6889

De Cruz P, *Comparative Law in a Changing World* (Routledge-Cavendish 2007)

Dworkin R, *Law's Empire* (Fontana 1986)

_, *Law's Empire* (Hart 1998)

Eco U, *Semiotics and the Philosophy of Language* (Indiana University Press 1986)

Estlund D, 'Beyond Fairness and Deliberation' in James Bohman and William Rehg (eds), *Democracy: Essays on Reason and Politics* (MIT 1997)

Evans N and Levinson SC, 'The Myth of Language Universals: Language Diversity and Its Importance for Cognitive Science' (2009) 32 Behavioral and Brain Sciences 429

Faure Y-A, 'Jeitinho and Other Related Phenomena in Contemporary Brazil' in Daniel Bach and Mamoudou Gazibo (eds), *Neopatrimonialism in Africa and Beyond* (Routledge 2013)

Gazal-Ayal O and Sulitzeanu-Kenan R, 'Let My People Go: Ethnic In-Group Bias in Judicial Decisions—Evidence from a Randomized Natural Experiment' (2010) 7 Journal of Empirical Legal Studies 403

Glenn HP, *Legal Traditions of the World: Sustainable Diversity in Law* (Oxford University Press 2010)

Graziadei M, 'Legal Transplants and the Frontiers of Legal Knowledge' (2009) 10 Theoretical Inquiries in Law 723

Hart HLA, *The Concept of Law* (Clarendon Press 1961)

Hegel GWF, *Phenomenology of Spirit* (JN Findlay ed, Oxford University Press 1979)

Hobsbawm E, *Nations and Nationalism since 1780: Programme, Myth, Reality* (Cambridge University Press 1992)

Kawata J (ed), *Comparing Political Corruption and Clientelism* (Ashgate Pub Co 2006)

Kazanavičiūtė R, 'Lithuania: Objectivity in Legal Discourse' < 'Australia's Academic and Research Network' <https://www.aarnet.edu.au> accessed 13 August 2016

Langacker R, *Foundations of Cognitive Grammar: Volume II: Descriptive Application* (Stanford University Press 1991)

_, *The Foundations of Cognitive Grammar: Volume I: Theoretical Prerequisites* (Stanford University Press 1999)

Legrand P, 'European Legal Systems Are Not Converging' (1996) 45 The International and Comparative Law Quarterly 52

_, 'Against a European Civil Code' (1997) 60 The Modern Law Review 44

Leiter B, 'Law and Objectivity' in Jules L Coleman, Scott Shapiro and KE Himma (eds), *The Oxford Handbook of Jurisprudence and Philosophy of Law* (Oxford University Press 2004)

Levinson SC, *Pragmatics* (Cambridge University Press 1983)

MacCormick N, *Legal Reasoning and Legal Theory* (Clarendon Press 1994)

_, 'Reasonableness and Objectivity' (1998) 74 Notre Dame Law Review 1575

_, *Rhetoric and The Rule of Law: A Theory of Legal Reasoning* (Oxford University Press 2005)

Orücü E, 'Comparative Law in Practice' in David Nelken and Esin Orücü (eds), *Comparative Law a Handbook.* (Hart 2007)

Owojori AA and Asaolu TO, 'The Role of Forensic Accounting in Solving the Vexed Problem of Corporate World' (2009) 29 European Journal of Scientific Research 183

Rawls J, 'The Idea of Public Reason' in William Rehg (ed), *Deliberative democracy: essays on reason and politics* (MIT 1997)

_, '"Justice as Fairness: Political Not Metaphysical", Philosophy and Public Affairs, 14 (3), Summer, 223-51' (1998) 97 International Library of Critical Writings in Economics 250

_, *Political Liberalism* (Columbia University Press 2005)

Reimann M, 'The Historical School against Codification: Savigny, Carter, and the Defeat of the New York Civil Code' (1989) 37 The American Journal of Comparative Law 95

Rorty R, *Richard Rorty: Philosophical Papers Set: Objectivity, Relativism, and Truth (Philosophical Papers, Vol. 1): Volume 1* (Cambridge University Press 1990)

Sacco R, 'Legal Formants: A Dynamic Approach to Comparative Law' (1991) 39 The American Journal of Comparative Law 343

Skoczeń I, 'Minimal Semantics and Legal Interpretation' [2015] International Journal for the Semiotics of Law -

Skorupski J and Wright C, 'Realism, Meaning and Truth' (1988) 38 The Philosophical Quarterly 500

Slapper G, *The English Legal System: 2012–2013* (Routledge 2012)

Štajnpihler T and Kristan A, 'Slovenia: Objectivity in Legal Discourse' <https://eprints.usq.edu.au/> accessed 11 June 2016

Stein P, *Legal Evolution: The Story of an Idea* (Cambridge University Press 2009)

Syme GJ, Nancarrow BE and McCreddin JA, 'Defining the Components of Fairness in the Allocation of Water to Environmental and Human Uses' (1999) 57 Journal of Environmental Management 51

Taruffo M, 'La Verità Nel Processo' [2012] Rivista Trimestrale di Diritto e Procedura Civile 1117

Taylor EH, 'H. L. A. Hart's Concept of Law in the Perspective of American Legal Realism' (1972) 35 The Modern Law Review 606

Tushnet M, *Weak Courts, Strong Rights Judicial Review and Social Welfare Rights in Comparative Constitutional Law* (Princeton University Press 2008)

Uviller R, 'Advocate, the Truth, and Judicial Hackles: A Reaction to Judge Frankel's Idea' (1975) 123 University of Pennsylvania Law Review 1067

Whalen-Bridge H, 'The Reluctant Comparatist: Teaching Common Law Reasoning to Civil Law Students and the Future of Comparative Legal Skills' (2008) 58 Journal of Legal Education

Wilson D and Sperber D, 'Relevance Theory' in Laurence R Horn and Gregory L Ward (eds), *The Handbook of Pragmatics* (Blackwell 2006)

Zirk-Sadowski M, 'Interpretation of Law and Judges Communities' (2012) 25 International Journal for the Semiotics of Law - 473

Zweigert K, *Introduction to Comparative Law* (Clarendon Press; Oxford University Press 1998)

Index

Studies in Politics, Security and Society

Edited by Stanisław Sulowski

Vol. 1 Robert Wiszniowski (ed.): Challenges to Representative Democracy. A European Perspective. 2015.

Vol. 2 Jarosław Szymanek: Theory of Political Representation. 2015.

Vol. 3 Alojzy Z. Nowak (ed.): Global Financial Turbulence in the Euro Area. Polish Perspective. 2015.

Vol. 4 Jolanta Itrich-Drabarek: The Civil Service in Poland. Theory and Experience. 2015.

Vol. 5 Agnieszka Rothert: Power of Imagination. Education, Innovations and Democracy. 2016.

Vol. 6 Zbysław Dobrowolski: Combating Corruption and Other Organizational Pathologies. 2017.

Vol. 7 Vito Breda: The Objectivity of Judicial Decisions. A Comparative Analysis of Nine Jurisdictions. 2017.

www.peterlang.com

www.ingramcontent.com/pod-product-compliance
Ingram Content Group UK Ltd.
Pitfield, Milton Keynes, MK11 3LW, UK
UKHW041827031026
15587UKWH00002B/616

9 783631 675908